ACCOUNTING

QuickStart Guide®

ACCOUNTING

QuickStart Guide®

The Simplified Beginner's Guide to Real-World
Financial & Managerial Accounting for Students,
Business Owners, and Finance Professionals

Josh Bauerle, CPA

Editor: Marilyn Burkley
Cover Illustration and Design: Katie Donnachie, Copyright © 2018 by ClydeBank Media LLC
Interior Design & Illustrations: Katie Donnachie, Copyright © 2018 by ClydeBank Media LLC

Third Edition - Last Updated: August 24, 2022

ISBN: 9781945051791 (paperback) | 9781945051784 (hardcover) | 9781945051494 (ebook) | 9781945051944 (audiobook) | 9781636100173 (spiral bound)

Publisher's Cataloging-In-Publication Data
(Prepared by The Donohue Group, Inc.)

Names: Bauerle, Josh.
Title: Accounting quickstart guide : the simplified beginner's guide to real-world financial & managerial accounting for students, business owners, and finance professionals / Josh Bauerle, CPA.
Other Titles: Accounting quick start guide
Description: Third edition. | Albany, NY : ClydeBank Finance, [2018] | Includes bibliographical references and index.
Identifiers: ISBN 9781945051791 (paperback) | ISBN 9781945051784 (hardcover) | ISBN 9781945051494 (ebook)
Subjects: LCSH: Accounting. | Bookkeeping.
Classification: LCC HF5636 .B38 2018 (print) | LCC HF5636 (ebook) | DDC 657--dc23

Library of Congress Control Number: 2018935094

Author ISNI: 0000 0004 6473 3553

For bulk sales inquiries, please visit www.clydebankmedia.com/orders, email us at orders@clydebankmedia.com, or call 888-208-6826. Special discounts are available on quantity purchases by corporations, associations, and others.

Copyright © 2018
www.clydebankmedia.com
All Rights Reserved

ISBN-13: 978-1-945051-79-1 (paperback)
ISBN-13: 978-1-636100-17-3 (spiral bound)

PRAISE FOR

QuickStart Guides

Really well written with lots of practical information. These books have a very concise way of presenting each topic and everything inside is very actionable!

— ALAN F.

My new book is so helpful, it's so easy to understand and I can recommend it to any client no matter what level of expertise they have (or don't have).

— AMANDA K.

Everything is written in a beautiful font which is great for people who get bored with reading.

— ANGEL L.

The book was a great resource, every page is packed with information, but [the book] never felt overly-wordy or repetitive. Every chapter was filled with very useful information.

— CUTRIS W.

I appreciated how accessible and how insightful the material was and look forward to sharing the knowledge that I've learned [from this book].

— SCOTT B.

My new QuickStart Guide is very easy to follow, it's really well written and it breaks everything down, especially the essentials.

— ARIZE O.

After reading this book, I must say that it has been one of the best decisions of my life!

— ROHIT R.

This book is one-thousand percent worth every single dollar!

— HUGO C.

The read itself was worth the cost of the book, but the additional tools and materials make this purchase a better value than most books.

— JAMES D.

This is a "go-to" book for not only beginners but also as a refresher for experienced practitioners.

— CHARLES C.

I finally understand this topic ... this book has really opened doors for me!

— MISTY A.

Contents

BEFORE YOU START READING,
DOWNLOAD YOUR FREE DIGITAL ASSETS!

 Sample Financial Statement Templates

 Helpful Accounting Ratio Cheat Sheet

 Business Plan Creation Tools for Entrepreneurs

 Easy Tax Treatment Cheat Sheet

TWO WAYS TO ACCESS YOUR FREE DIGITAL ASSETS

Use the camera app on your mobile phone to scan the QR code or visit the link below and instantly access your digital assets.

 SCAN ME

or — www.clydebankmedia.com/accounting-assets

🖥 **VISIT URL**

Introduction

I never expected to like accounting. I was not even introduced to the subject voluntarily but rather was required to take the course during my senior year at Kent State University. Like most unwilling accounting students, I would rather have ~~forfeited a limb~~ taken some other course, any other course, really—history of bowling, tofu sculpture, patternmaking for dog garments.[1] But it was accounting that stood between me and my diploma. So I took accounting—and loved it.

In retrospect, my taking to accounting like a fish to water should have been foreseeable. I grew up obsessed with sports statistics. While my childhood friends watched sports to follow the unfolding fortunes of their favorite players and teams, I was watching—with equal enthusiasm—to find out how the latest results would impact batting averages, pass completion percentages, and earned run averages.

During my first accounting class, it hit me: accounting is essentially the practice of generating and analyzing statistics for businesses. Instead of tracking target batting averages, we track target net incomes. Instead of home run to strikeout ratios, we track asset to liability ratios. Moreover, the drama of business is often sufficient to rival that of sports, and accountants are key players in the middle of it all.

Looking back on my time as a student, I must give credit where it is due. The fact that I had an extraordinary professor definitely helped open my eyes to the possibility that accounting could be something other than a punishing prerequisite to graduation, but could be instead an enjoyable and worthy professional pursuit. Professor McFall is one of Kent State's best, and his enthusiasm for the craft of accounting went a long way toward inspiring my career in this field. I do expect that the time I spent under Professor McFall's tutelage will carry over into this text, much to the benefit of you, the reader.

It was thanks in large part to Professor McFall's course that I decided to change my major to accounting, even though doing so as a senior meant adding another two years to my college career (sorry, Mom and Dad!). Within a few years of earning my undergraduate degree and gaining some experience as a professional **accountant**, I completed the requisite graduate-level coursework, and I sat for the exams required to become a CPA.

While holding the CPA (certified public accountant) designation is nice insofar as it signifies the topmost level of expertise in the field, its main benefit is the peace of mind it provides to those seeking accounting services. Why? Let me tell you a secret—anyone can call themselves an accountant, even if they are not a CPA, even if they hold no degree at all. But for an individual or business in need of accounting support, the CPA designation acts as a public vote of confidence, because it verifies that the accountant possesses a significant level of education, experience, and board-certified licensing.

Obviously, there is a long road between newbie accounting student and CPA. And for many students the first few miles on this road can be disorienting, even grueling.

Here are a few incredibly simple but valuable pieces of advice, especially relevant if you are a pure beginner in this field:

» Patience is key.
» It gets easier.
» You can do it! (You might even enjoy it.)

Speaking of beginners, this QuickStart Guide was written to be understandable by those who have zero to very little accounting knowhow. This includes newly enrolled accounting students as well as business owners, managers, bookkeepers, and others in the professional world seeking knowledge of accounting fundamentals.

I've found that newcomers to accounting require a *lot* of encouragement. At the college level, Intro to Accounting is often seen as a "weed out" course, a trial-by-fire for the undergraduate. Accounting is regarded with similar dread in the professional world. Many business owners view it as an arcane endeavor, practiced by strange and humorless creatures (accountants). These same business owners, as much as they would like to clarify their tax burdens and exert greater control over their business's finances, are reluctant to take time out of their schedules to learn basic accounting themselves. That is a mistake.

I could tell you countless horror stories of clients who failed to grasp the importance of proper accounting in their businesses and ended up paying a big price for it. I could tell you about Linda (all names changed to protect the guilty), who failed to properly reflect her rental property in her accounting records and as a result paid over $15,000 in taxes she would not have had to pay otherwise. Or Dave, whose multimillion-dollar sale of his business fell through because his accounting records were so poor the purchaser decided the numbers could not be trusted. With so much at stake, why doesn't every business owner and manager learn basic accounting?

One popular reason for avoiding accounting—prevalent in both the academic and business communities—is fear of math. People assume accounting requires the use of complex mathematics, and that those with average or subpar math skills will quickly lose their footing. Others put off learning accounting not because they are scared of the math, but because they do not believe that accounting can be learned outside of a classroom setting, so they see no reason to pursue an independent study or purchase a book such as this one. Still others, hailing from the opposite end of the misperception spectrum, believe that accounting is nothing more than glorified budgeting, and if you know how to use a calculator and maybe a spreadsheet or two, then you are totally equipped to work as a chief financial officer (CFO).

They are wrong, on all accounts (no pun intended). For starters, accounting centers on the organization of financial data; it has very little to do with any exotic mathematics. The main challenges you will face at the beginner level are conceptual, not quantitative. Second, you can definitely establish a very strong foundational and even advanced-level knowledge of accounting by way of independent study. Beginning with the book you are currently reading, there are a vast number of resources available to anyone willing to take advantage of them. There are several free searchable accounting websites that cover most any accounting topic under the sun. There are also virtual classroom-style learning opportunities.

Accounting is a skill and requires study. Learning accounting is like learning a language, the "language of business." It is a language that is universal and incredibly useful. To succeed in your independent study of this subject you must be patient, persistent, and optimistic. You will need to put in some solid hours of study. Certain fundamental accounting concepts that I will introduce in this book will not seem intuitive at first. You will need to warm up to them, and I will be doing my best to break the ice for you, using simple explanations and examples to help make your study as smooth, efficient, and valuable as possible. You will be surprised and pleased with the return you get for your efforts.

Accounting skills prove very useful in a multitude of scenarios. I have listed a few here:

> » **Loan shopping** – Want to raise some money for your start-up? Or maybe you already have a proven business model and want to scale up before a swarm of copycats beats you to the punch. Banks, lenders, and other investors appreciate accurate, properly prepared financial statements. Speak their language. Get funded!

» **Starting a new job (or improving competency at your current job)** – If you were hired to do bookkeeping or other financial work, a strong grasp of accounting fundamentals will make you much more proficient at your job. Understanding the fundamentals contained in this book can give you the confidence to widen your realm of responsibility at work or even to ask for a raise.

» **Rectifying cash flow problems** – One of the most common problems businesses encounter—often leading them to seek help from a CPA like myself—is cash flow. In many cases, business seems to be moving at a decent pace, yet the bank account balance keeps shrinking. Basic accounting can help business owners monitor their financial activity and root out and correct cash flow problems.

» **Fraud prevention** – You may not know this, but smaller businesses lose a lot more from fraud than do larger business (relative to their total incomes).[2] To prevent fraud, larger businesses often spread accounting responsibilities out over multiple parties and even departments. In small businesses, it is often only one or a few persons controlling the books. If the owner or manager of the business has a fundamental understanding of accounting principles, then there is more opportunity for oversight and fraud prevention efforts.

» **Tax planning** – Taxes are the fundamental concern for many of my clients. Good accounting allows businesses to clarify and thereby minimize their tax burdens. They pay on time, penalty-free, and no more than what's required by law.

» **Self-employment** – In the modern "gig economy," 30 percent of the national workforce is self-employed.[3] Whether you are an Uber driver, a real estate broker, or a freelance graphic designer, an understanding of basic accounting will help you better manage your business activity and tax obligations.

» **Day-by-day business decision-making** – From Amazon and Etsy sellers to brick-and-mortar donut shop owners, better control of finances leads to better business decision-making. Take, for instance, the value of accurate and timely financial statements. If you are a small business owner with a lot of cash coming in and going out, it can be difficult to determine how much money you are actually making. Maybe you are considering buying a new house or car, or perhaps your teenager is headed to college soon, and you need to take some money out of the business. Basic accounting knowledge will help you zero in on the value of your equity holdings. You will know how much money you actually have and how much you can safely withdraw.

One final note before we dive into the content, structure, and theory behind this text: I would like to invite students who are pursuing college-level accounting coursework to make use of this text as a primer for what you will be encountering in the classroom. If you can find the time to read and study this book end to end, then you will surely possess a significant advantage. If you have a penchant for the schadenfreude that comes from watching others struggle to get their heads around concepts that you have already mastered, then this book will truly enhance your classroom experience! Enjoy!

Chapter by Chapter

Accounting encompasses several dimensions, the main branches being "financial accounting" and "managerial accounting" (the differences between the two are explained in chapter 1). While there are plenty of full-length textbooks devoted exclusively to financial accounting and others devoted to managerial accounting, I have attempted to include in this text the most useful and essential introductory concepts from each universe. For readers more interested in practical and immediate business applications of accounting concepts, you will find ample material throughout the text that will help you gain greater control over your business's financial mechanics. I *do not* advise skipping the financial accounting chapters on the assumption that they offer little practical application for the day-by-day activities of a small business. In fact, many of the examples presented in the financial accounting chapters revolve around the working realities of small businesses (as well as large ones).

As far as charting a course for your reading, my belief is that students, entrepreneurs, bookkeepers, etc. will benefit from reading this book straight through and learning the concepts in the order in which they are presented. Since this is meant to be a beginner-level book, I have refrained from unnecessarily delving too deep into any given concept for the sake of showcasing my own knowledge. The objective throughout is to produce opportunities for learners to gain knowledge of fundamental accounting concepts as simply and clearly as possible.

In case you are still not convinced that a straight-through reading is in your best interest, I provide brief chapter summaries here to guide your reading choices:

» "Chapter 1: Accounting as a Tool of Business" – This chapter explores some of the major business-related reference points used frequently in accounting, such as business entity types and the three main kinds of business activity. The chapter also introduces the four main branches of accounting.

» "Chapter 2: Introduction to Financial Statements" – This chapter introduces common financial statements as well as other essential accounting concepts, such as accrual vs. cash-basis accounting and the use of fiscal years.

» "Chapter 3: Financial Statement Analysis" – This chapter explores how certain metrics and formulas can be used to analyze financial statement data. Some common methods of asset depreciation are also introduced.

» "Chapter 4: Assets = Liability + Equity" – This chapter introduces the fundamental accounting equation (assets = liabilities + equity) and explains why it is the basis for the widely used "double-entry" accounting system. Chapter 4 also explains in detail the critical concept of debits and credits.

» "Chapter 5: Recording Business Transactions" – The accounting methods introduced in this chapter support organizational structures and protocols that keep accounting systems accurate and intelligible.

» "Chapter 6: Managerial Accounting: How to Put Accounting Fundamentals to Work on Behalf of Your Business" – This chapter covers a broad range of managerial accounting concepts including cost-volume-profit analysis (CVP analysis), budgeting, and multi-product analysis.

» "Chapter 7: Using Financial Accounting to Select and Monitor Stocks and Other Investments" – While the primary intent of this chapter is to showcase accounting as a useful tool for investment selection, perhaps more useful for accounting students is the chapter's detailed review of GAAP (generally accepted accounting principles).

» "Chapter 8: Income Tax Accounting, or Keeping Your Business Out of IRS Crosshairs" – This chapter provides a summary-level look at the critical role played by the accountant in the tax services industry. The anatomy and logic of the progressive income tax system is also detailed in this chapter.

» "Chapter 9: Detecting and Preventing Fraud" – This chapter is a chronicle of dark deeds performed by unscrupulous office personnel. It explains how accountants sniff out fraud while minimizing fraud incentive and opportunity.

» "Chapter 10: Sizing Up the Software for Accounting and Bookkeeping" – This chapter provides a look at the ever-present technological components of accounting, including when to implement new software and how to define selection criteria.

|1|
Accounting as a Tool of Business

Behind every good business is a good accountant.

– ANONYMOUS

(probably an accountant)

An online retailer, let's call her Kathi, who sells jewelry to customers all over the world, is considering hiring five new employees to help her expand her business. Kathi would like to offer these new employees fair and competitive compensation but is unsure of how much she can afford to pay them on an ongoing basis. Last month, Kathi moved her jewelry business out of her basement and rented a workshop and retail space in a midtown shopping center with heavy foot traffic. Paying rent every month is an added business expense, but having a new walk-in customer base to supplement online sales will (Kathi hopes) provide a strong boost to the business's revenue.

In the same shopping center, a print shop owner/franchisee, let's call him James, has been operating at a small loss for the last four months. At a recent national conference the print shop owner met other franchisees who claimed to have restored profitability to their businesses by eliminating certain product and service offerings. James is now studying his sales records, looking for products and services that do not generate enough revenue to justify their expense.

Meanwhile, the print shop owner's franchise-issuing parent company, a multibillion-dollar publicly held corporation, has had a very profitable quarter and would like to return some of that money to its shareholders in the form of dividend payments. But how much can the company afford to pay out? It depends on how much cash needs to remain on hand to effectively continue normal business operations and to make new investments that will help grow the business.

From newly-minted online retailers to Fortune 500 companies, fundamental accounting practices pave the way for informed and optimal decision-making. A strong grasp of basic accounting gives business decision-makers access to more precise, more relevant, and more actionable information.

Good accounting practice is also a matter of good financial maintenance. In every business there are accounting-related matters that need to be taken care of each month (or more often). A business well-inoculated against fraud will routinely balance its books and promptly investigate any discrepancies. A business that cares about its bottom line will regularly produce and review financial statements that aid in analyzing profit and loss. Businesses also use accounting to evaluate sales data, employee performance, investment opportunities, and a whole lot more. Even if you don't have a resident bookkeeper in your company or a CPA on retainer, much of the power of accounting can be harnessed with simple-to-use accounting software, a subject we will be covering in more depth later on in this book. But first, since this is a QuickStart Guide and intended to be beginner-friendly, we're going to begin at, well, the beginning.

Business Entity Types

One of the beautiful things about the subject of accounting is that the core concepts are readily applicable across a wide variety of business types. From online shoe retailers to industrial steel smelters, and from LLCs to S corporations, the fundamentals of good accounting do not change. Nevertheless, the selection of a legal structure for your business does have consequences, and certain of these consequences, namely the tax implications, will affect the way you manage your books. Sole proprietorships, partnerships, limited liability companies (LLCs), and corporations are all examples of legal structures, or business entity types.

In addition to affecting the way your business will be taxed, several other factors are affected by your choice of legal structure, including the following:

> » **Legal standing** – Some entity types, such as sole proprietorships and partnerships, have a legal standing that is essentially synonymous with the business's owner(s). Corporations, by contrast, are treated as independent entities that can assert their own legal standing; a corporation can sue another corporation or an individual.

» **Liability** – Just as a corporation can sue by virtue of its own legal standing, it can also be held liable and be sued. In corporations and LLCs (limited liability companies), owners may enjoy a level of insulation from liabilities incurred by the business; not so with sole proprietorships and partnerships.

» **Costs of formation and ongoing administration** – Partnerships and sole proprietorships are cheap and easy to set up and administer; LLCs and corporations require more of an investment.

Let's take a look at each business entity type (legal structure) more closely.

Sole Proprietorship

A sole proprietorship is automatically created as soon as a business owner begins transacting business. This legal structure is the simplest to establish and the easiest to administer. It is also, in many cases, the riskiest. The owner/proprietor is personally liable for all obligations, financial and otherwise, legally incurred by the business. If the business is sued, then technically the owner is being sued. If the business is drowning in debt, then the owner's personal assets may be at risk.

The business's profits are treated as "pass-through" income and are reflected in the proprietor's personal tax filings.

Partnership

As the name suggests, a partnership is composed of two or more people who establish a business and share in its profits, losses, and liabilities in accordance with a partnership agreement. Similarly to a sole proprietorship, profits and losses are "passed through" to the partners to report on their own individual income tax returns.

Good accounting practices in a partnership help to ensure that ownership of profits from the business are accurately recorded through the use of "owner's capital" accounts, which we will discuss in the following chapter.

Corporation

Corporations are generally classified as "S corporations" or "C corporations." For small businesses, the S variety is more common, while C corporations are typically larger businesses. Ownership of corporations is defined by publicly or privately issued shares. As a business entity, corporations are separate from the individual(s) who own it. Corporations possess their own legal status and incur their own liabilities. If a corporation is sued and forced to pay a settlement, the shareholders are not required to foot the bill.

In C corporations, the corporation is taxed as an entity unto itself *and* the shareholders are taxed on their capital gains and dividend income. This "double taxation" can be avoided by opting instead for an S corporation. In an S corporation, corporate earnings become "pass-through" income and are only taxed at the shareholder level.

LLC (Limited Liability Company)

The LLC, which is growing in popularity, allows owners to enjoy benefits of both a corporation and a partnership. In an LLC, like an S corporation, profits and losses are passed through to owners without taxation of the business itself, and owners may be shielded from personal liability. The differences between LLCs and S corporations are highly technical in nature: for example, LLCs have managers, whereas S corps have a board of directors; S corps may reduce self-employment tax liability; and S corps may only have 100 shareholders, whereas LLCs may have an unlimited number of members.

LLCs and other business entity types are discussed in greater detail in ClydeBank Media's *LLC QuickStart Guide.*[4]

We will revisit business entity types in chapter 8, when we conduct an entity-by-entity comparison of the tax burdens incurred on a hypothetical net income of $100,000.

The Three Parts of Business Activity

This is interesting: did you know that all businesses, regardless of their legal structure, perform only three essential functions? While such a pronouncement may overlook a great deal of diversity and complexity, in some sense it's 100 percent true, at least as far as your accountant is concerned. Business activity can be reduced to three categories: financing, investing, and operating.

Financing

A business's financing activities involve the acquisition of capital. Business owners can self-finance their business by contributing their own money. They may also seek outside investments and loans from banks or other lenders.

Financing, though especially important in the early stages of a business's development, is also important throughout the life of the business. The acquiring and servicing of debt allows businesses to establish confidence among lenders and bondholders. Businesses with better credit ratings can acquire capital less expensively than businesses with poor ratings. Easier and cheaper access to capital means greater expansion and investment opportunity.

When a business issues and sells stock in exchange for *equity* (ownership) shares in the business, it is known as "equity financing." When a business takes on loans or issues bonds, it is known as "debt financing."

Investing

A business's investing activity is the acquisition of assets to be applied toward the operation of the business. If Kathi decided to purchase new equipment for her jewelry repair workshop, that would be an example of an investment. Businesses can also invest in real estate, computers, insurance policies, and any number of other assets to aid in business operations.

Operating

A business's operating activity is its normal business activity. It usually revolves around the inflow of *revenue* and the outflow of *expense*—the selling of products or services and the payment of bills. Expenses differ from investments because they are short-term in nature and usually do not involve the company's acquisition of significant assets. The rent Kathi pays monthly for her midtown retail space is an expense, but if she had *purchased* the property to use as her storefront, it would constitute an asset. The importance of this distinction (expense vs. asset) will become clear as you continue your study of the principles of accounting.

The Role of Accounts in Tracking Business Activity

An *account* is a record that displays the culmination of certain transactions. Every account can be classified as an *asset*, *liability*, *equity value*, *revenue*, or *expense*.

As shown in figure 1, underneath each major account type are listings of several actual accounts. The nature of the business and its financial management approach will determine which accounts it uses. An account can be defined under any major account type at the discretion of the business owner. If a pet shop owner wants to keep a separate account for all revenues that come from the sale of goldfish, there is no rule that says he cannot establish a goldfish revenue account.

fig. 1

ASSET ACCOUNTS	REVENUE ACCOUNTS	EQUITY ACCOUNTS
Cash	Sales Revenue	Common Stock
Accounts Receivable	Service Revenue	Owner's Capital
Land	Interest Revenue	Contributions
Property	Licensing Revenue	Dividends
Equipment	Other Revenue	Retained Earnings
Inventory		Other Equity Accounts
Copyrights		
Patents		
Other Asset Accounts		

THE 5 MAIN ACCOUNT TYPES

LIABILITY ACCOUNTS	EXPENSE ACCOUNTS
Loans Payable	Rent Expense
Accounts Payable	Supplies (short-term)
Salaries & Wages Payable	Cost of Goods Sold
Bonds Payable	Licensing Expense
Other Liabilities	Utility Expense
	Insurance Expense
	Other Expenses

For beginner-level students of accounting, it is not important at this point to have an exact understanding of all the many different accounts and how they interrelate with one another. That understanding will come as we progress further through this QuickStart Guide. For now, let's work on building a basic understanding of the five main account types listed in figure 1. One way to develop such an understanding is to explore how these account types can be associated with the three main business activities discussed previously in this chapter.

There is no exact or formal association between the various business activity types and account types. But when it comes to understanding how the different account types function, it can be helpful to use business activity type as a point of reference.

Take, for instance, financing activity. Financing activity is particularly relevant to a business's *liability accounts*. Liability accounts record and quantify upcoming financial obligations. When a business pursues financing by taking out a loan from a bank, the business incurs a liability. The amount of the loan is recorded by the business (via an accountant, a bookkeeper, or accounting software) in a liability account. When payments are made on the loan, the value of that account is reduced (debited). Simultaneously, the amount of cash taken out of the business's bank account to make the payment on the loan results in a reflexive adjustment to the "cash account." The value of the cash account is reduced (credited).

Financing activity can also be relevant to a business's *equity accounts*. Equity accounts quantify the value of various ownership interests in the business. When a business owner writes a check to help finance her business, the value of the owner's capital contributions account (an equity account) goes up. Similarly, when a corporation procures capital investment by selling stock to shareholders, the value of stockholder equity (also an equity account) goes up.

Investing activity is particularly relevant to a business's *asset accounts*. Asset accounts record and quantify the financial value of a company's assets. They might include cash, land, property, equipment, inventory, copyrights, patents—essentially anything inherently valuable that the business owns. Accounts receivable—money owed to the business—is also considered an asset account even though its ultimate value depends on the future payments of outside parties.

When a business makes a new investment it usually means acquiring more assets, which is why investing activity will, in most cases, have some effect on the business's asset accounts. When Kathi buys her new jewelry repair equipment for her workshop at a price of $5,000, her equipment account (an asset account) will increase by $5,000 and her cash account (also an asset account) will decrease by $5,000.

Another possibility for Kathi is that she does not pay cash but instead finances her purchase of the new equipment, in which case her asset account would still increase by $5,000 but, instead of a decrease to her cash account, her *accounts payable* account would be *increased* in the amount of $5,000. Accounts payable is not an asset account but a liability account, which indicates that money is owed.

REMEMBER

When a business engages in financing activities, its liability accounts will usually be affected.

Operations activity is particularly relevant to a business's revenue and expense accounts. As previously stated, the essence of business operations is the inflow of revenue and the outflow of expense. Revenue accounts may include sales revenue, service revenue, and a variety of other accounts which track how the business is bringing in money. Expense accounts may include rental payments, cost of goods sold, business travel expense, and a variety of other accounts which track how money leaves the business during routine operations.

Revenue and expense accounts are central to the creation of a business's income statement, one of the four major financial statements used in accounting, all of which will be discussed in detail in chapters 2 and 3.

Branches of Accounting

Kathi, the jewelry store sole proprietor mentioned at the beginning of this chapter, has a need for accounting. She needs to make sure that she is taking in revenue sufficient to cover her expenses and that she has enough cash on hand to pay down her debts. She needs accounting to identify areas of the business in need of attention and to ward off any unpleasant surprises come tax season.

Compare Kathi's accounting needs to those of an investment bank considering the acquisition of a new company, or those of the IRS exploring new methodologies for more effective and efficient audits, or those of an FBI agent investigating organized crime. The nature of the "accounting need," so to speak, varies substantially.

There are several different branches of accounting, including auditing, forensic accounting, and government accounting. For now, however, I would like you to focus on the four most essential and prevalent accounting branches: bookkeeping, financial accounting, managerial accounting, and income tax accounting.

Bookkeeping

Bookkeeping is the simplest but perhaps most fundamentally vital dimension of accounting. The job of a *bookkeeper* is to collect and record data and to do so accurately. While accountants may be charged with organizing and presenting financial data in a useful way, the role of data collection extends well beyond the role of the accountant. Data is collected by cashiers, secretaries, interns ... and that is just the beginning. The janitor in your office building collects and reports inventory data about available cleaning supplies. The production assistant who works at the film studio records the costs of props and set pieces. A business hires bookkeepers to centralize and organize data being collected throughout the company. A bookkeeper may update and maintain basic reports and financial statements.

Were we to venture a little off the deep end in an effort to romanticize the role of the accountant, we might say that the bookkeeper is responsible for keeping the armory supplied (with accurate financial data) for use by the accountant, who employs these tools as needed in the field of battle (and by battle I mean financial business analysis and other distinctly danger-free endeavors).

Accounting software, which we will discuss in more depth in chapter 10, has become an indispensable tool for bookkeepers. Much of it is easy to use and capable of generating standard financial statements.

Financial Accounting for External Parties

Financial accounting focuses on the preparation of financial data, statements, etc., for interested parties outside of the business or organization. When a corporation reports its financials to investors, or when a small business presents its financial records to a bank in hope of securing a loan, these are examples of financial accounting.

Other examples of external users of financial data include prospective business partners. If an LLC is considering allowing a new member to buy in to the business, the prospective partner (and his attorney) will first want to review the company's financial records. In this instance, financial accounting is used to help aid in an important business decision (whether or not to join the company) and to help determine a fair buy-in price. For similar reasons, financial accounting is also prevalent in the world of mergers and acquisitions of all sizes.

A large produce company, FruitCorp, is looking for smaller produce companies to acquire. FruitCorp decides to target companies with weaker earnings but substantial assets, especially property assets such as warehouses and real estate. FruitCorp's primary objective is to expand its warehousing capacity and to further decentralize its distribution. The acquisitions team believes that produce companies with weaker earnings will be willing to sell off their businesses at lower prices, and FruitCorp will thus be able to acquire their assets at a discount.

Q: Which two financial statements will FruitCorp's acquisition team definitely rely on when evaluating prospective acquisitions?

Answer: The targeted companies, if interested in a buyout, will be asked to provide their income statements and balance sheets. FruitCorp's acquisition team will use the income statements to assess the strength of the companies' earnings and will use the balance sheets to assess the nature and value of their assets, particularly property and real estate. This is financial accounting at work.

Financial accounting statements tend to be less detailed than the statements used in managerial accounting (see the following section). When a business is disclosing its financial data to an outside party, there is an incentive to craft the statement in such a way as to hide proprietary information about the company. You want the outside party to get a clear sense of the business's financial health, but you do not necessarily want to disclose intricate details about the business's accounts, such as the names of key vendors or creditors. Financial accounting statements are also not issued as frequently as managerial accounting statements, generally speaking.

We will revisit financial accounting throughout this text, particularly in chapter 7, where we will be discussing the use of financial accounting when selecting and monitoring investments.

Managerial Accounting for Internal Parties

Managerial accounting is essentially everything financial accounting is not. *Managerial accounting* is the discrete, strategic, detailed, and frequent financial reporting used in day-to-day business activities. At the beginning of this chapter, we introduced James, a sole proprietor who owns a print shop franchise in the same midtown shopping center where Kathi crafts jewelry. James's dilemma centered on his store's recent lack of profitability, as shown on his income statements. Following his attendance at a conference, where he met other franchisees facing similar challenges, James resolved to conduct rigorous inspections of his product and service offerings and to weed out unjustified expenses.

One such service identified by James was high-volume commercial printing, a service facilitated by a gargantuan, space-age contraption known as the IBM Infoprint 2085, with a price tag of $30,000. James had elected not to invest in the machine, but instead to lease it for a monthly sum of $592 (an annual expense of $7,104). After reviewing twelve months' worth of itemized sales reports, James determined that the high-volume commercial printing service was costing his business more than it was generating in revenue. Through the use of managerial accounting, James came to the conclusion he needed to either raise the price of the service or discontinue it altogether.

James's approach to his dilemma is an example of managerial accounting in action. Managerial accounting involves the use of accounting principles to inform decision-making within a company's internal management apparatus. Like good financial accounting, good managerial accounting begins with good bookkeeping. Without accurate source data, the conclusions of managerial accounting would be useless or even counterproductive.

In addition to choosing which services to continue, cancel, and change, managerial accounting has a host of other business applications, including the following:

» Deciding how to structure promotions or coupon offerings
» Analyzing customer demographics
» Deciding how to package and present products
» Determining appropriate payment for employees and contractors
» Establishing budgets
» Determining methods of employee evaluation
» Deliberating on investment decisions
» Qualifying customers for credit

One of the things I really like about managerial accounting is that it is a space in which accountants can showcase their creativity. One of the key roles of the CFO is to shape managerial accounting systems, reports, statements, and strategies in such a way that they align with the unique needs of the business. Indeed, many businesses have managerial accounting systems so specialized and so prized that they are closely guarded and treated as valuable intellectual property.

Many of the reports and financial statements used in managerial accounting are similar to those used in financial accounting. Typically, in managerial accounting, financial statements are produced with more frequency and more detail and are more likely to be customized for the purpose of informing business decision-making.

You will undoubtedly find business managers eager to inspect their income statements (profit/loss statements) to get a look at their bottom line. But you will also come across other report formats that center around the evaluation of employees, the success of a product, or the timeline for a construction project. Another unique aspect of managerial accounting is that, unlike financial accounting, reports may be built using non-monetary data. An inventory report, the results of a massive customer survey, an amalgamated record of employee performance reviews conducted over the previous ten years (why you would ever want such a report I do not know)—all of it falls under the purview of managerial accounting.

We will be revisiting managerial accounting throughout this text, especially in chapter 6.

Many accounting texts and courses focus exclusively on either managerial or financial accounting. This book aims to provide elements of both, while offering practical insight for both business owners and students of accounting.

Income Tax Accounting

In my experience as a ***certified public accountant (CPA)***, tax compliance and tax strategy are what truly motivate small business owners/managers to keep organized and accurate books. The purpose of income tax accounting is to ensure businesses pay their taxes in full and on time and thereby avoid tax penalties and possible prosecution.

The accounting practices required of businesses by the IRS can be quite different from those used in financial or managerial accounting. The latter methods, particularly those of financial accounting, are standardized by a system known as GAAP, the Generally Accepted Accounting Principles. The US Securities and Exchange Commission—which regulates the buying and selling of financial securities such as stocks and bonds—legally requires publicly traded companies to use GAAP. Many private companies voluntarily adhere to GAAP, though they are not legally bound to do so. The essential purpose of GAAP is to ensure that everyone is on the same page when it comes to financial reporting. Adherence to GAAP prevents companies from manipulating formulas and definitions for the purpose of sculpting and cherry-picking the data they would prefer to feature on their financial reports. Interested parties, such as prospective lenders or investors, are thus able to come to reliable conclusions about the company's financial well-being.

A company goes public and sells its stock shares on the open market. The company's adherence to GAAP gives the stock's prospective buyers confidence that the company's financial reports were created using an intelligible, reliable, and objective methodology.

Tax accounting is covered in more detail in chapter 8. The main principles and "assumptions" of GAAP are reviewed in chapter 7. If your primary interest in accounting is tax-related, then I would recommend adding ClydeBank Media's best-selling book, *Taxes for Small Businesses QuickStart Guide*[5] to your reading list.

HANDS-ON LEARNING: For more information on forensic accounting, auditing, and government accounting, be sure to check out my online course. Visit www.clydebankmedia.com/accounting-assets

Chapter Recap

» The selection of a business's legal structure is important in determining how the business is taxed, how it incurs liabilities, and how owner equity is accounted for.

» Business activities can be grouped into three main categories: financing, investing, and operating.

» An account can be defined as the recorded value of a given business asset, liability, equity value, revenue, or expense.

» Accounting is a multifaceted discipline, with bookkeeping, financial accounting, managerial accounting, and tax accounting forming the major branches.

| 2 |

Introduction to Financial Statements

Chapter Overview
» Financial Statements
» The Fiscal Year
» Accrual vs. Cash Accounting

If accounting is the language of business, then financial statements are a translating tool used to relay information from the world of accounting to the world of business decision-making. You don't have to be an accountant to make extraordinary use of financial statements. CFOs and bookkeepers are hired (and paid well) to produce these statements so that executives, owners, managers, and shareholders can make intelligent decisions based on sound financial data.

These are the four most basic and widely used financial statements:

» Income statement
» Statement of owner's equity
» Balance sheet
» Statement of cash flows

In this chapter we will introduce these statements and discuss how they relate to one another.

The Income Statement
Also known as the profit/loss or PL statement, the *income statement* lists the business's revenues and expenses over a given time period. The main output of the income statement is the business's *net income* (total revenues minus total expenses). You may also hear net income referred to as "income," "profit," or "earnings." On an income statement, both revenues and expenses

are broken down by account type, such as "sales revenue" and "service revenue" (for revenue accounts) and "rent expense" and "insurance expense" (for expense accounts). Here is a sample income statement for Kathi's Jewelry Design.

fig. 2

KATHI'S JEWELRY DESIGN
Income Statement
For the Month Ending on 11/30/17

Revenues				
Online sales revenue	$	5,900		
Brick-and-mortar sales revenue	$	2,300		
TOTAL REVENUES			$	8,200
Expenses				
Rent expense	$	2,500		
Wage expense	$	1,800		
Advertising expense	$	1,000		
Supplies expense	$	450		
Insurance expense	$	70		
TOTAL EXPENSES			$	5,820
Net income			$	2,380

Many income statements for smaller businesses like Kathi's will only have one revenue account. But because Kathi is in a unique situation—attempting to expand her formerly online-only business into an online/brick-and-mortar hybrid—she has separated her income into two revenue accounts.

The net income for Kathi's business in November is $2,380. This figure will be relayed to the statement of owner's equity.

Statement of Owner's Equity

Kathi ran her jewelry business as an online-only enterprise for five years before deciding to rent her midtown storefront. Though her monthly income statements show an occasional net loss, she usually operates at a profit and has accumulated enough profit to offset her losses over time. Kathi pays herself monthly by transferring cash from the business's checking account to her personal checking account (this is known as an "owner's withdrawal"). In order to build more equity in the business, Kathi tries to keep her monthly payments to herself less than the business's net profit. In November 2017, for example, even though the business's net profit turned out to be $2,380, Kathi only paid herself $2,000, which added $380 to her equity share in the business. This $380 is what was left over after the employees were paid, after the bills were paid, and even after Kathi was paid. This money will still be kept in the business's bank account, but for accounting purposes it belongs to the owner and is tracked in an account called "owner's equity."

Owner's equity is the owner's claim on the assets of a business. Simply put, it is the dollar amount of the business's wealth that technically belongs to the owner or owners. Owner's equity is what is left over after all the business's liabilities are accounted for. As of October 31, 2017, Kathi has $19,200 in owner's equity (see the first line on the sample statement of owner's equity in figure 3).

fig. 3

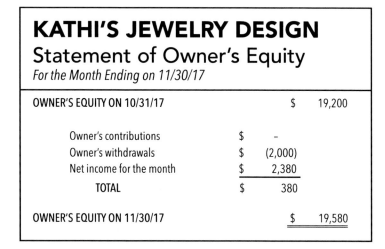

KATHI'S JEWELRY DESIGN
Statement of Owner's Equity
For the Month Ending on 11/30/17

OWNER'S EQUITY ON 10/31/17	$	19,200
Owner's contributions	$	–
Owner's withdrawals	$	(2,000)
Net income for the month	$	2,380
TOTAL	$	380
OWNER'S EQUITY ON 11/30/17	$	19,580

The *statement of owner's equity* is used to report owner's equity for a given period of time. The layout of the statement is rather simple, as there are only four main variables that must be accounted for:

» The previous, or beginning, equity balance
» The net income recorded for the given period
» Owner contributions
» Owner withdrawals

The statement is generally composed of "plus" entries and "less" entries. Plus entries show increases in owner's equity, that is, owner contributions and net income. Net losses and owner's withdrawals are less entries, since they reduce owner equity. Kathi's statement, as depicted in figure 3, blends plus and less entries into one *total* value for the period (showing the total change to owner equity). You may come across other versions of statements of owner's equity that list and total all plus entries separately from all less entries. Since Kathi's statement is for a small sole proprietorship and covers a very short accounting period (one month), our simplified and streamlined statement will suffice.

In a sole proprietorship like Kathi's Jewelry Design, the main equity account is the owner's capital balance—the equity Kathi holds in the business. When a business forms as a corporation, issues stock, and has shareholders, then the shareholder's equity, rather than the owner's equity, becomes the most important equity account. Furthermore, when a corporation records a profit on its income statement, it may wish to issue dividend payments to its shareholders. Rather than create a statement of owner's equity, the corporation may instead create a **retained earnings statement**, which outputs the quantity of net income retained following the issuance of dividend payments to stockholders. See chapter 3, Financial Statement Analysis, for a walk-through example of how a retained earnings statement is created.

It helps to have your various financial reports defined according to the same period of time. If your income statement is for the fiscal year 2018, then your statement of owner's equity should adhere to that same time period, as you need to carry your business's net income from the former report and add it to the plus section in the latter.

The main output from the statement of owner's equity is the owner's equity value at the end of the defined term. In our figure 3 example, that number is $19,580. Another name for this output is the "end-of-period capital balance." The end-of-period capital balance for one period is always the beginning or "opening" capital balance for the next period; for example, $19,580 will be listed at the top of Kathi's statement of owner's equity for the month ending on December 31, 2017. In this way, owner's equity remains fluid and traceable from period to period.

The end-of-period capital balance is used to configure the balance sheet, which is the next financial statement we will discuss.

NOTE

If Kathi had one or more business partners, then the statement of owner's equity for Kathi's Jewelry Design would be more complex, with separate ledger entries for each owner equity account.

Balance Sheet

The balance sheet encapsulates one of accounting's most important principles:

ASSETS = LIABILITIES + EQUITY

(aka *"the fundamental accounting equation"* see chapter 4)

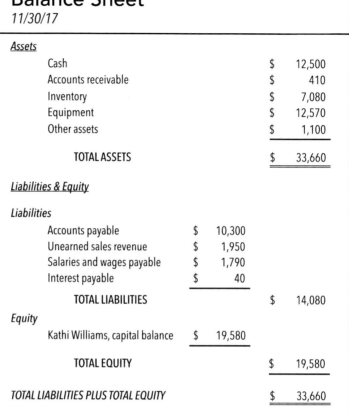

KATHI'S JEWELRY DESIGN
Balance Sheet
11/30/17

Assets		
Cash	$	12,500
Accounts receivable	$	410
Inventory	$	7,080
Equipment	$	12,570
Other assets	$	1,100
TOTAL ASSETS	$	33,660

Liabilities & Equity				
Liabilities				
Accounts payable	$	10,300		
Unearned sales revenue	$	1,950		
Salaries and wages payable	$	1,790		
Interest payable	$	40		
TOTAL LIABILITIES			$	14,080
Equity				
Kathi Williams, capital balance	$	19,580		
TOTAL EQUITY			$	19,580
TOTAL LIABILITIES PLUS TOTAL EQUITY			$	33,660

GRAPHIC

fig. 4

In figure 4, notice how the total value of all of the business's assets ($33,660) is equal to the combined total value of the business's liabilities and equity ($14,080 + 19,580 = $33,660).

The balance sheet is so named because asset value, when properly rendered, will always equal the sum of total liabilities and total equity. Whenever the balance sheet for a business is unbalanced, it means that there is an accounting error somewhere in the books that needs to be resolved. The internal logic of the balance sheet will become clearer during our study of the fundamental accounting equation in chapter 4.

Balance sheets are distinct from other financial statements in that they capture only a snapshot (rather than a defined period) of time. Income statements, statements of owner's equity, and cash flow statements tell the story of a given *period* of time. By contrast, a company's **balance sheet** tells its managers where the company stands financially at a given moment in time.

Balance sheets are generally issued at the end of a significant period, such as a quarter or a ***fiscal year***. A fiscal year can be defined simply as any twelve-month period that ends on the last day of a month but does not end on December 31. Businesses may elect to use fiscal years (rather than calendar years) for accounting and tax purposes. Kathi and other retailers, for instance, might elect to use a fiscal year ending on the last day in February, considering that March is traditionally accompanied by a decline in retail sales following the Christmas season and Valentine's Day.

However, fiscal years are more commonly used by larger C corporations than by sole proprietorships (like Kathi's), partnerships, LLCs, and S corporations. Larger companies are given a little more leeway. But smaller companies are certainly entitled to state their case for using a fiscal year, and they can do so using IRS Form 1128, *Application to Adopt, Change, or Retain a Tax Year.*

The owner of a fireworks company travels to China every September for a giant international trade show, where over 70 percent of the company's inventory is purchased for the year, including a massive amount of product that will be retailed during the following year's Fourth of July season. The owner of the company files IRS Form 1128 requesting a fiscal year ending July 31, on the basis that the expenses incurred in September are closely related to the revenues earned in June and July of the following year. Using a calendar year to track tax liability and finances would leave the business's books lacking in continuity.

The essential structure of the balance sheet does not change regardless of whether the business uses a calendar year or a fiscal year. A listing of the business's assets, liabilities, and equity will always be featured. What may change from balance sheet to balance sheet is the format. The balance sheet in figure 4 is known as the "report form." It lists all of the assets on top and the liabilities and equity on the bottom. Another format for the balance sheet is known as the "account form," where all of the assets are listed on the left and liabilities and equity are listed on the right (figure 5).

A "left/right" formatting or visualization of accounts, with the assets on the left and the liabilities and equities on the right, is used frequently in accounting, not only on balance sheets. The reason for this formatting will be made clear in chapter 4 when we discuss debits and credits.

Notice the equity account, "Kathi Williams, capital balance." This is the "end-of-period capital balance" we discussed in the previous section, the main output we get from the statement of owner's equity.

KATHI'S JEWELRY DESIGN
Balance Sheet
11/30/17

fig. 5

Assets			Liabilities & Equity				
Cash	$	12,500					
Accounts receivable	$	410	**Liabilities**				
Inventory	$	7,080	Accounts payable	$	10,300		
Equipment	$	12,570	Unearned sales revenue	$	1,950		
Other assets	$	1,100	Salaries and wages payable	$	1,790		
			Interest payable	$	40		
			TOTAL LIABILITIES			$	14,080
			Equity				
			Kathi Williams, capital balance	$	19,580		
			TOTAL EQUITY			$	19,580
TOTAL ASSETS	$	33,660	*TOTAL LIABILITIES PLUS TOTAL EQUITY*			$	33,660

In the current snapshot of time, as reflected in the balance sheet, Kathi would have $19,580 left over after settling all of her liabilities. A slight alteration in the fundamental accounting equation allows us to visualize an important truth about business: Assets – Liabilities = Equity. Years ago, when I took my first accounting course, I asked my professor why the fundamental accounting equation is not, by default, expressed as Assets – Liabilities = Equity. The answer can be found in the principles of left/right accounting (liabilities and equity must be shown on the right) which, as previously mentioned, will be explained in detail in chapter 4. Nevertheless, Assets – Liabilities = Equity is indeed a true expression, just not as practically useful for accounting purposes as Assets = Liabilities + Equity.

Unlike the income statement, statement of owner's equity, and statement of cash flows, the balance sheet does not have an output number. The balance sheet is used not only to sniff out accounting errors (when the balance sheet does not balance), but also to evaluate the financial health of the company. Kathi's business, for instance, has just over $30,000 in assets, enough to cover her liabilities (debts) two times over. Nevertheless, Kathi has only $12,500 in cash. If all of her liabilities ($14,080) became due at once, let's say on December first, then it would be impossible for her to pay.

It is the accountant's job to use the balance sheet to analyze critical financial issues facing a business, such as the nature of the business's debt, the liquidity of its assets, and the ongoing sustainability of its cash position.

Statement of Cash Flows

The *statement of cash flows* clarifies the inflow and outflow of cash over a given period of time and is used to ensure that the company retains enough cash on hand to expediently service its debts while not keeping so much cash on hand that its risk of fraud or theft is significantly elevated.

The statement of cash flows is organized in alignment with the three main business activities discussed earlier in this chapter; there are cash flows from operating activities, cash flows from investing activities, and cash flows from financing activities.

fig. 6

KATHI'S JEWELRY DESIGN
Statement of Cash Flows
For the Month Ending on 11/30/17

Cash Flows from Operating Activities		
Cash flows from sales	$ 6,760	
Outgoing cash from operating activities	$ (5,650)	
NET CASH FLOW FROM OPERATIONS		$ 1,110
Cash Flows from Investing Activities		
Equipment purchase	$ (4,905)	
NET CASH FLOW FROM INVESTING		$ (4,905)
Cash Flows from Financing Activities		
Owner's withdrawal	$ (2,000)	
NET CASH FLOW FROM FINANCING		$ (2,000)
Net Cash Flow		$ (5,795)
Cash position at the beginning of the period		$ 18,295
Current cash position		$ 12,500

The sample statement of cash flows in figure 6 covers the same period (the month of November 2017) as that covered by the income statement and the statement of owner's equity depicted in figures 2 and 3, respectively. Immediately beneath the statement heading are Kathi's cash flows from operating activities. Cash coming in from sales *as well as cash going out* to pay employees, rent, supplies, etc. are all reported as cash flows from operating activities.

Were you to compare Kathi's cash flows from operating activities (figure 6) with her income statement from the same period (figure 2) then you might wonder why the *net income* on the income statement differs from the *net cash flow from operations* on the cash flow statement. On her November income statement, Kathi reports total sales revenue of $8,200 but only reports $6,760 in cash received from sales in November. Similarly, Kathi reports a total of $5,820 in accrued expenses on her income statement but reports a cash outflow of only $5,650 for the same period. How do we explain these discrepancies?

The answer can be found in the concept of **accrual basis accounting**. For beginner-level students, understanding the difference between accrual basis accounting and **cash basis accounting** is critical. In accrual basis accounting, transactions are recorded as soon as any debt is incurred, regardless of whether cash has in fact changed hands. Revenue is thus reported on the basis of when the business performs a service or sells a product—regardless of when payment is received. Expenses are recorded on the basis of when the expenses are incurred—regardless of when payment is made. If Kathi sells $1,500 worth of product in November to customers on a payment plan—underwritten by Kathi's business—then, using accrual accounting, the value of those sales are still recorded as income in the November period, even though Kathi has yet to receive any cash payment. Similarly, if Kathi puts $200 worth of supplies on the company credit card in November, under the accrual method those purchases are still November expenses, even though the credit card bill will not be paid until December or January.

Cash basis accounting, by contrast, tracks all revenue and expenses on the basis of cash flow. The $200 worth of supplies that Kathi puts on her credit card in November will be recorded as a December or January expense (depending on when she pays her credit card bill), and the $1,500 worth of financed sales will not count toward November sales revenue, because the cash was not received in November.

Back to our original question. The reported net income (found on Kathi's income statement) does not match the net cash flow from operations (found on Kathi's statement of cash flows) because she created her income statement using accrual basis accounting.

Accrual basis accounting is preferred by many businesses because it offers more accurate and immediate information about their financial performance. Cash accounting, though it offers a more immediate awareness of the business's actual cash position, may create a certain level of distortion if relied upon to reflect actual financial activity. Nonetheless, in the real world most small businesses end up using cash basis accounting because of the relative simplicity of record keeping.

NOTE

C corporations that generate over $5 million a year in sales are required by the IRS to use accrual basis accounting. Also, businesses that maintain product inventories *and* do over a million in sales are required by the IRS to use accrual basis accounting.

Businesses with inventories that do under a million in sales can use cash basis accounting, so long as they don't deduct the costs of their inventories from their net profits.

An optimal practice is to use accrual basis accounting alongside a well-maintained statement of cash flows. Doing so will allow you to simultaneously track and utilize the most relevant and immediate financial data while keeping a close eye on your cash balances.

Cash flows from investing activities track outgoing cash resulting from the purchase of equipment, real estate, or other long-term assets. Kathi's purchase of new equipment for her business falls outside the scope of normal business operating activities and is recorded instead as a negative cash flow resulting from investment activities.

The third section of the statement of cash flows tracks cash flows from financing activities. When a company issues stock or bonds, the cash received from these issues is reported under the financing activities section of the statement of cash flows. This section is used by smaller businesses to track not only outside financing activities but owner financing activities as well. If the owner writes a check to the business, the activity is recorded as an "owner contribution." If, as in Kathi's case, the owner withdraws money from the business, this activity is recorded as an "owner's withdrawal" (see figure 6).

How Financial Statements Are Interrelated

A trained accountant, when provided with the requisite source material, should be able to construct accurate and useful financial statements. Depending on the nature and size of the company, the type of accounts used to construct financial statements will vary widely. The fundamental structure of each, however, is more or less universal. Every balance sheet, for example, should have a section for assets, liabilities, and equity, with assets equal to liabilities plus equity. Every statement of cash flows should delineate operating activities, investing activities, and financing activities. Every income statement should offer a record of a business's revenues plotted against its expenses for a given period, with net income as the output.

The relationships between certain inputs and outputs of same-period financial statements is also a constant. Figure 7 is a simple diagram illustrating the essential connection points between financial statements.

If you feel confident in your understanding of financial statements by this point, great! And if you are still unclear on certain details, don't be alarmed. Financial statements are an expansive topic. We will explore in more depth their construction and real-world application in chapter 3 and throughout this text.

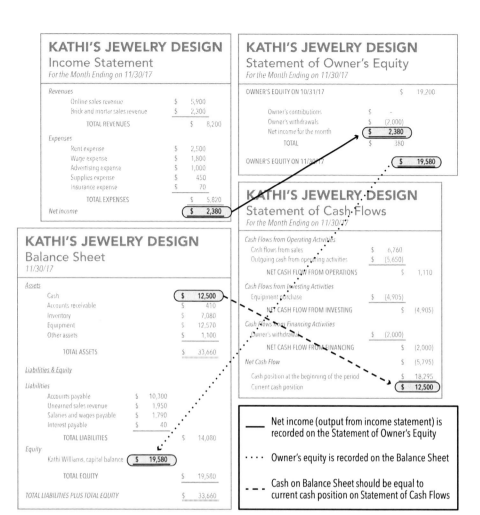

KATHI'S JEWELRY DESIGN
Income Statement
For the Month Ending on 11/30/17

Revenues
Online sales revenue	$	5,900
Brick and mortar sales revenue	$	2,300
TOTAL REVENUES		$ 8,200

Expenses
Rent expense	$	2,500
Wage expense	$	1,800
Advertising expense	$	1,000
Supplies expense	$	450
Insurance expense	$	70
TOTAL EXPENSES		$ 5,820
Net income		$ 2,380

KATHI'S JEWELRY DESIGN
Statement of Owner's Equity
For the Month Ending on 11/30/17

OWNER'S EQUITY ON 10/31/17		$ 19,200
Owner's contributions	$	-
Owner's withdrawals	$	(2,000)
Net income for the month	$	2,380
TOTAL	$	380
OWNER'S EQUITY ON 11/30/17		$ 19,580

KATHI'S JEWELRY DESIGN
Balance Sheet
11/30/17

Assets
Cash	$	12,500
Accounts receivable	$	410
Inventory	$	7,080
Equipment	$	12,570
Other assets	$	1,100
TOTAL ASSETS		$ 33,660

Liabilities & Equity

Liabilities
Accounts payable	$	10,300
Unearned sales revenue	$	1,950
Salaries and wages payable	$	1,790
Interest payable	$	40
TOTAL LIABILITIES		$ 14,080

Equity
Kathi Williams, capital balance	$	19,580
TOTAL EQUITY		$ 19,580
TOTAL LIABILITIES PLUS TOTAL EQUITY		$ 33,660

KATHI'S JEWELRY DESIGN
Statement of Cash Flows
For the Month Ending on 11/30/17

Cash Flows from Operating Activities
Cash flows from sales	$	6,760
Outgoing cash from operating activities	$	(5,650)
NET CASH FLOW FROM OPERATIONS		$ 1,110

Cash Flows from Investing Activities
Equipment purchase	$	(4,905)
NET CASH FLOW FROM INVESTING		$ (4,905)

Cash Flows from Financing Activities
Owner's withdrawal	$	(2,000)
NET CASH FLOW FROM FINANCING		$ (2,000)
Net Cash Flow		$ (5,795)
Cash position at the beginning of the period		$ 18,295
Current cash position		$ 12,500

_____ Net income (output from income statement) is recorded on the Statement of Owner's Equity

. . . . Owner's equity is recorded on the Balance Sheet

- - - Cash on Balance Sheet should be equal to current cash position on Statement of Cash Flows

GRAPHIC

fig. 7

Chapter Recap

» Financial statements organize and summarize account information to reveal important financial realities facing a business or organization.

» Businesses may use fiscal years rather than calendar years for tax and other accounting purposes.

» Cash basis accounting is based on the actual arrival and departure of cash into and out of the business; accrual basis accounting is based on the accrual of payable and receivable obligations.

| 3 |
Financial Statement Analysis

Chapter Overview
» Income Statement Applications
» Retained Earnings Statements
» Multiyear Income Statements
» Calculating Earnings Per Share
» Current and Long-Term Accounts
» Liquidity and Solvency Ratios
» Depreciation
» Free Cash Flow

The three most dreaded words in the English language are 'negative cash flow.'
— DAVID TANG

In this chapter we will dive deeper into the anatomy and applications of the income statement, balance sheet, and statement of cash flows. These financial statements are central to both financial and managerial accounting. Though incredibly useful in their own right, each has shortcomings that can obfuscate the full financial picture. They function best when used together. This is why accountants aim to unify the production of financial statements around specific, consistent, agreed-upon time periods, so as to allow timely and reliable apples-to-apples comparisons.

The financial statements featured in the previous chapter were those of a sole proprietorship, Kathi's Jewelry Design. In this chapter we will follow the financial story of a much larger corporate business entity called PrintCo. The majority of accounting principles carry over quite evenly from one type/ size of business to the next, at least in terms of how financial information is categorized and presented—the "bookkeeping" level, if you will. The "accounting" level—how we derive actionable meaning and intelligence from available financial information—becomes more nuanced in response to variations in business type and size.

The Ins and Outs of the Income Statement

In chapter 2, we reviewed the income statement for Kathi's Jewelry Design, a small sole proprietorship. Income statements, in the context of Kathi's business, are fairly straightforward. Every business owner is interested in whether her revenues exceeded her expenses, and thus whether or not the business made a profit or incurred a loss. Recall James, our other entrepreneur, who relied on his income statements to zero in on areas of his business that were generating too much expense without enough revenue to compensate. If you recall, James is an owner/franchisee of a much larger corporate chain: a publicly traded company that we'll call PrintCo. And like James and Kathi, PrintCo is in the business of making profits and relies on income statements to track its success. Let's take a look at a simplified income statement from PrintCo (figure 8).

fig. 8

PrintCo
Income Statement
For the Year Ending on 12/31/17 (all dollar amounts in millions)

Revenues		
Sales revenue	$ 9,867	
TOTAL REVENUES		$ 9,867
Expenses		
Cost of goods sold	$ 4,719	
Selling/General/Admin expense	$ 3,080	
Depreciation/Amortization	$ 105	
Income tax expense	$ 698	
TOTAL EXPENSES		$ 8,602
Net income		$ 1,265

PrintCo's income statement shows $1.27 billion in net income. Because PrintCo is a publicly traded company, it has the option of returning some of its profits to its investors in the form of dividend payments. This transaction is recorded in the company's retained earnings statement. Had PrintCo, in anticipation of turning a $1.27 billion profit, decided to issue $300 million worth of dividend payments to its stockholders, then its retained earnings statement might look something like this (figure 9):

GRAPHIC

fig. 9

PrintCo
Retained Earnings Statement
For the Month Ending on 12/31/17 (all dollar amounts in millions)

Retained Earnings as of January 1	$	680
Plus: Net income	$	1,265
	$	1,945
Less: Dividends issued	$	300
Retained Earnings as of December 31	$	1,645

The story of the retained earnings statement is simple. PrintCo had $680 million worth of retained earnings at the beginning of 2017. They posted a 2017 profit of $1.27 billion and paid out $300 million in dividends, leaving them with $1.65 billion in retained earnings at the end of the year.

REMEMBER

Retained earnings is net income that is retained for use within the business. For accounting purposes it is handled similarly to owner's equity; it is reported on the balance sheet (we will show you how this is done later in this chapter).

Existing and prospective stockholders use retained earnings statements to assess the frequency and generosity with which a company issues dividend payments. Though there are plenty of investors who are attracted to companies with a reputation for paying generous dividends, there are others who prefer to invest in companies that pay fewer dividends and use more of their net income to invest in new growth opportunities.

We have shown how an income statement is used by a business owner for managerial accounting purposes (through the experiences of Kathi and James) and we have shown how an income statement with a retained earnings statement can be used by a company's prospective and current stockholders.

Since stockholders are considered outside parties, this application would be an example of financial rather than managerial accounting. Can you think of any other applications for the income statement?

What about for tax purposes? By virtue of cataloging both taxable revenues and deductible expenses, a business's income statement can be very handy come tax time (see chapter 8).

Another common application of the income statement is the comparison of year-by-year data.

GRAPHIC

fig. 10

PrintCo
Income Statements
2015 - 2017 (all dollar amounts in millions)

	2017	2016	2015
Revenues			
Sales revenue	$ 9,867	$ 11,354	$ 7,364
TOTAL REVENUES	$ 9,867	$ 11,354	$ 7,364
Expenses			
Cost of goods sold	$ 4,019	$ 5,105	$ 3,565
Selling/General/Admin expense	$ 3,120	$ 3,420	$ 2,730
Depreciation/Amortization	$ 765	$ 805	$ 830
Income tax expense	$ 698	$ 820	$ 624
TOTAL EXPENSES	$ 8,602	$ 10,150	$ 7,749
Net income/loss	$ 1,265	$ 1,204	$ (385)

Year-by-year data such as that featured in figure 10 provides another example of how income statements can present data that is useful from both a managerial and a financial accounting perspective. Executives at PrintCo may be eager to investigate why sales revenue from 2016 was approximately $2.5 billion higher than it was in 2017. Meanwhile, prospective creditors and stockholders may be interested in the fact that the company's successive 2016 and 2017 profits were sufficient to recover its 2015 losses six times over.

Another possible point of interest from the stockholder's perspective is the use of reported net income or loss to calculate *earnings per share (EPS)*. Earnings per share is the amount of income generated by a company divided by its outstanding shares of stock. If you had a company with ten shareholders, each holding one share, and the company made $100 in profit, then the company's EPS would be $10.

EPS is important to stockholders because it offers a reliable way to compare different periods of performance, usually on a year-by-year basis.

This type of comparison, involving the evaluation of a single company over successive periods of time, is known as an ***intracompany comparison***, whereas the comparison of different companies is known as ***intercompany comparison***.

EPS is useful for intracompany comparisons, but because the quantity of shares issued by different companies can vary drastically (especially among smaller and medium-sized corporations), the use of EPS for intercompany comparisons is not generally useful.

In the preceding example with the ten shareholders dividing $100 in profit among them, the formula we used for calculating EPS was simply net income/loss divided by total shares outstanding. For a stock broker, this level of detail may suffice, but for an accountant charged with reporting a company's financial records while complying with GAAP, things get a little more complicated. A more formal formula for EPS can be expressed as follows:

fig. 11

$$\text{EARNINGS PER SHARE} = \frac{\text{NET INCOME} - \text{PREFERRED DIVIDENDS}}{\text{WEIGHTED AVERAGE OF OUTSTANDING COMMON STOCK SHARES}}$$

There are a few components in the figure 11 formula that may not be familiar to a beginner-level student of accounting. "Preferred dividends," for example, refers to dividend payments issued to preferred stockholders.

Earnings per share, unless otherwise specified, refers to earnings per share of *common*, not preferred, stock. The intricacies of common vs. preferred stock are not integral to accounting and not within the scope of this text. For extensive coverage of that topic, please see ClydeBank Media's QuickStart Guide to Investing.[6]

Preferred stock dividends are subtracted from the net income because the numerator in our formula is meant to reflect all net income available to common stockholders. Preferred stockholders have priority when it comes to dividend and other payouts from the company; therefore, any money earmarked for preferred stockholders cannot be considered when calculating earnings per share of common stock.

Notice, too, that the denominator in the figure 11 formula, when figured properly, is a weighted average; this as opposed to relying on the most recently reported quantity of outstanding common stock shares. The accountant's formula must be more precise, more exacting. We use the weighted average within a given period to account for the fact that quantities of outstanding shares continually change.

Returning to PrintCo's income statement for 2017 (figure 8), let's assume there were 675 million outstanding shares of PrintCo stock on January 1, 2017, and 750 million shares of stock on December 31, 2017. Let's also assume that the company is not paying any dividends to preferred stockholders.

To calculate EPS, we first acknowledge that, since no preferred stock dividends were paid during the period, our numerator is simply our net income (earnings), $1.27 billion. For the purposes of this beginner-level text, we will use our two data points, January 1 and December 31, to make a simplified calculation of the approximate weighted average of outstanding common stock shares during 2017.

$$\frac{675 + 750}{2} = 712.5 \text{ M}$$

Let's assume that 712.5 million is our weighted average of outstanding shares of common stock in 2017. Our EPS, therefore, is 1 dollar and 78 cents per share.

$$\frac{1.27 \text{ B}}{712.5 \text{ M}} = \$1.78$$

EPS is useful primarily from a financial accounting perspective, as it allows intracompany comparisons at the stockholder level. From a managerial accounting perspective, the simplest and most relevant intracompany comparison is made by assessing net income or loss on a year-by-year basis.

It is important to note that money raised from the issuing of stock does not constitute revenue on the income statement, nor does the payment of dividends constitute an expense. Each of these transaction types are recorded in the company's equity accounts and can be visualized on the balance sheet.

Putting It in Perspective with the Balance Sheet

Let's take a look at the balance sheet for PrintCo. Obviously, the accounting will be more complex in a multibillion-dollar corporation, but at the end of the day, the principles are the same as those used in smaller businesses. Total assets must be equal to the sum of total liabilities and total equity. The equity accounts can be compared with the liability accounts in order to assess and quantify competing claims on the company's assets—in figure 12, both equity and debt holders hold an approximately $3.1 billion dollar claim on PrintCo's $6.3 billion in assets.

PrintCo
Balance Sheet
12/31/17 (all dollar amounts in millions)

GRAPHIC

fig. 12

Assets				*Liabilities*				
Cash and cash equivalents	$	1,924		Accounts payable	$	1,286		
Accounts receivable	$	1,540		Notes payable	$	955		
Other current assets	$	230		Other current liabilities	$	334		
TOTAL CURRENT ASSETS			$ 3,694	TOTAL CURRENT LIABILITIES			$	2,575
Property	$	1,209		Long-term debt	$	463		
Equipment	$	415		Other long-term liabilities	$	98		
Long-term investments	$	765		TOTAL LONG-TERM LIABILITIES			$	561
Other assets	$	198						
TOTAL LONG-TERM ASSETS			$ 2,587	TOTAL LIABILITIES			$	3,136
TOTAL ASSETS			$ 6,281	*Equity*				
				Stockholder equity	$	1,500		
				Retained earnings	$	1,645		
				TOTAL EQUITY			$	3,145
				TOTAL LIABILITY PLUS EQUITY			$	6,281

Larger companies, and occasionally smaller ones as well, parse out the assets and liabilities on their balance sheet into long- and short-term categories. Long-term assets, such as property and equipment, are different from short-term ones in that they are not as easily liquidated. Not only would the selling of property or equipment require locating a buyer, but it would also potentially threaten the company's ability to continue its business operations. If you sell the factory, then where will you make your products? This is why long-term assets warrant their own grouping on the balance sheet. Though they may possess real value, they cannot actively support the business's immediate financial needs.

NOTE

In some circumstances a business may want to use its long-term assets as collateral when pursuing new debt financing.

The technical threshold that delineates a ***current asset*** from a ***long-term asset*** is the expectation that the company will convert the asset into cash within a year's time. Similarly, if the asset is not likely to become cash within a year, then it is properly considered a long-term asset.

This one-year threshold is also in play on the liability side of the balance sheet. Debts that are not expected to be paid within a year's time are grouped as **long-term liabilities** and debts payable within the year are **current liabilities**.

While one year is the most common threshold for separating current and long-term assets and liabilities, certain companies and industries may use an interval longer than one year for current assets, so as to adequately reflect the length of the company's **"operating cycle."** The operating cycle of a vineyard, for example, is longer than one year because the planting, the harvesting, the storing/aging, and the selling of product spans more than a year's time. Therefore, even though a barrel of wine may need sixteen months to ferment and age before it can be sold, it is still considered a current asset.

Executives, as well as potential investors and lenders, use balance sheet components to gauge a company's financial well-being. For example, when assessing the ability of a company to service its short-term obligations, its current liabilities are compared with its current assets. This is known as the **current ratio**:

$$\text{CURRENT RATIO} = \frac{\text{CURRENT ASSETS}}{\text{CURRENT LIABILITIES}}$$

The current ratio for PrintCo on December 31 is 3,694/2,575, or 1.43. A current ratio over 1 means that the company has liquidity sufficient to settle all of its short-term debts on the spot. An ideal current ratio would be 2 or above, indicating that the company has liquid assets sufficient to cover its current liabilities twice over. A current ratio of 2 means that there is very little risk that the company will need to lean on any long-term assets or take out additional financing in order to fund its near-term obligations.

The current ratio is a type of liquidity ratio. **Liquidity ratios** are those aimed at evaluating a company's ability to meet its short-term financial obligations. In addition to the current ratio, there are several other liquidity ratios used in accounting, including the "quick ratio" and the "cash ratio" (figure 13).

In addition to liquidity ratios, working capital is often used to measure liquidity. **Working capital** is defined as a company's current assets minus its current liabilities. A negative working capital balance is a red flag, indicating that the company may be at risk of defaulting on its debts.

QUICK RATIO	HOW TO EVALUATE
$$\text{QUICK RATIO} = \frac{\text{CASH + AR +}}{\text{CURRENT LIABILITIES}}$$ **MARKETABLE SECURITIES** **Current assets** are assets a company holds that should be fairly easy to convert into cash within a year's time. **Current liabilities** are short-term debts, usually payable within a year.	The quick ratio is similar to the current ratio but includes only highly liquid assets as opposed to all current assets. A quick ratioof at least 1 is therefore more assuring than a current ratio of the same value.
CASH RATIO	HOW TO EVALUATE
$$\text{CASH RATIO} = \frac{\text{CASH}}{\text{CURRENT LIABILITIES}}$$	The cash ratio is "quicker" than a quick ratio, as it only considers cash assets. A cash ratio of 1 is more assuring than a current or quick ratio of the same value.

GRAPHIC

fig. 13

An exceptionally high working capital balance is not always a good thing either. Companies with steadily increasing working capital balances often have too much money tied up in inventory (a current asset) or may be failing to efficiently collect on accounts receivables (also a current asset).

Just as liquidity ratios and working capital are used to evaluate a company's ability to service short-term debts, *solvency ratios* are used to evaluate the strength of a company's long-term financial position. One example of a commonly used solvency ratio is the ***debt-to-asset ratio***, which compares total liabilities to total assets:

$$\text{DEBT TO ASSETS RATIO} = \frac{\text{TOTAL LIABILITIES}}{\text{TOTAL ASSETS}}$$

The debt-to-asset ratio is a percentage measurement of the extent to which a company's assets are financed by creditors. Based on PrintCo's balance sheet from December 31, the company has a debt-to-asset ratio of about 50 percent, meaning that creditors have a claim on half of the company's assets. There is a zero-sum relationship between creditors and equity holders when it comes to claims; the greater the claim exerted by creditors over a company's assets, the more ground is lost and the more risk is assumed by equity holders. If the company becomes insolvent and declares bankruptcy, the creditors are always paid first.

The equity section of PrintCo's balance sheet differs significantly from that of Kathi's Jewelry Design (see figure 4). In Kathi's balance sheet, the owner's capital balance, $19,580, is imported from the statement of owner's equity. In PrintCo's balance sheet, the corporation's retained earnings, about

$1.6 billion, is imported from its retained earnings statement (figure 9) and is added to stockholder equity.

In the PrintCo balance sheet, the stockholder equity account is worth $1.5 billion, meaning simply that PrintCo has raised $1.5 billion through the issue of stock, a "financing" activity.

NOTE

The value of the stockholder equity account has nothing to do with the current market price of the company's stock. A company's stock price is determined solely by investor demand. The value of the company's stockholder equity account is simply a measure of capital acquired through the issuing of stock.

REMEMBER

Capital acquisitions through stock issues are recorded as equity accounts. Capital acquisitions through debt issues (loans, bonds) are recorded as liabilities.

A simple way to understand the difference between the equity accounts of a corporation and the equity accounts of a sole proprietorship, partnership, LLC, or similarly structured business is to envision the following variations of the fundamental accounting equation:

FOR A CORPORATION:
ASSETS = LIABILITIES + (COMMON STOCK + RETAINED EARNINGS)

FOR A SOLE PROPRIETORSHIP:
ASSETS = LIABILITIES + OWNER'S EQUITY

The recording of retained earnings and common stock as equity accounts on the balance sheet may confuse some newcomers to accounting. Recall the retained earnings statement, shown again in figure 14.

Retained earnings can be defined as the net income remaining after dividends are paid out to stockholders. Keep in mind that the stockholders still legally own the corporation's retained earnings. Retained earnings is thus rightfully classified as an equity account and is positioned as such in the "corporate" rendering of the fundamental accounting equation: Assets = Liabilities + (Common Stock + Retained Earnings).

The common stock component simply tracks the influx of capital from stockholders. When a corporation issues stock, the buyers of the stock provide the company with cash. The corporation increases its cash (asset account) balance and increases its common stock (equity account) balance. The equation remains, as always, in balance.

To frame things in another way, the corporation's retained earnings are ultimately derived from the business's operating activities, whereas the corporation's common stock account value is derived from the business's financing activities.

Sole proprietorships, partnerships, and LLCs have no need to distinguish retained earnings from common stock, because these entity types do not issue stock and do not pay dividends. The owner(s) may withdraw or contribute capital at any time and in any amount.

fig. 14

PrintCo
Retained Earnings Statement
For the Month Ending on 12/31/17 (all dollar amounts in millions)

Retained Earnings as of January 1	$	680
Plus: Net income	$	1,265
	$	1,945
Less: Dividends issued	$	300
Retained Earnings as of December 31	$	1,645

In chapter 2 we looked at the statement of owner's equity from Kathi's sole proprietorship. That statement is depicted here again in figure 15.

fig. 15

KATHI'S JEWELRY DESIGN
Statement of Owner's Equity
For the Month Ending on 11/30/17

OWNER'S EQUITY ON 10/31/17	$	19,200
Owner's contributions	$	–
Owner's withdrawals	$	(2,000)
Net income for the month	$	2,380
TOTAL	$	380
OWNER'S EQUITY ON 11/30/17	$	19,580

In our example, the owner (Kathi) already had $19,200 worth of equity in the business before the month of November. For the average small business owner, $19,200 is a considerable amount of money to leave in the business unless you are planning on making a major investment of some kind in the near future. In my experience as an accountant, most business owners like to withdraw as much as they can from the business at the end of each period. And I don't blame them. Why use your business as a bank when you could withdraw the money and park your excess cash in a high-yield savings account? On the other hand, some business owners open up savings accounts in their business's name to generate interest income while they're saving up for a new piece of equipment or new property. Once the equipment or property is purchased, it becomes a business asset and is reflected as such on the balance sheet.

Speaking of equipment purchases, it is important to understand how depreciation is factored into certain assets that appear on the balance sheet. When a business makes a large investment to acquire a particular asset to satisfy longer-term needs—like a vehicle, technology, or a piece of heavy equipment—the business may break up the cost of the asset into fragments and report each fragment as an expense on several successive income statements and tax filings.

A self-employed professional gamer invests in a $2,000 state-of-the-art gaming PC so he can record gameplay of the latest, most advanced video games. The purchase is considered a legitimate business investment, but rather than immediately record the entire $2,000 purchase price as an expense, the gamer decides to depreciate his new asset over a four-year period, claiming $500 in expenses each year following the purchase.

When assets are depreciated, their cost minus the accumulated depreciation are still reported on the business's balance sheet.

Let's take a look at the assets section of the PrintCo balance sheet after the accumulated depreciation of equipment has been properly recorded (figure 16).

Notice that the total value of PrintCo's equipment asset account in figure 16 ($415 million) is identical to the value of the equipment account in figure 12. We have simply unpacked the depreciation details by accounting for the original cost of equipment ($865 million) and adding an accumulated depreciation account that shows $450 million in equipment depreciation as of December 31, 2017.

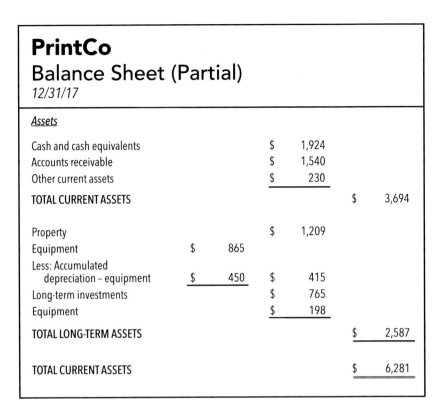

PrintCo
Balance Sheet (Partial)
12/31/17

Assets

Cash and cash equivalents			$	1,924	
Accounts receivable			$	1,540	
Other current assets			$	230	
TOTAL CURRENT ASSETS					$ 3,694
Property			$	1,209	
Equipment	$	865			
Less: Accumulated depreciation – equipment	$	450	$	415	
Long-term investments			$	765	
Equipment			$	198	
TOTAL LONG-TERM ASSETS					$ 2,587
TOTAL CURRENT ASSETS					$ 6,281

GRAPHIC

fig. 16

Methods of Depreciation

A lot of judgment calls need to be made when you're choosing how to depreciate your assets. Some assets should be depreciated more quickly than others. Some assets may have their entire purchase price depreciated over time, while others can only be depreciated partially.

A few asset types, such as land, cannot be depreciated, because they do not lose their value over time. Also, any property that is placed in the service of a business but is not used for more than one year cannot be depreciated. If the business invests in stocks or bonds, these assets cannot be actively depreciated because their value is always determined by their market price.

NOTE

The IRS establishes some basic asset categories and accompanying guidelines for depreciation in Publication 946.

Some assets can only be depreciated to a certain baseline level, because they will always possess some level of market value. A vehicle, for instance, even though it may lose a lot of value, will usually still be resalable, even after years of use, for parts if nothing else.

Before we begin to depreciate an asset we must first identify the base value for that asset. This base value is sometimes referred to as the "*residual value*," or "salvage value."

Straight Line Depreciation

Straight line depreciation is the simplest depreciation method. Let's say I buy a $5,000 computer server system for use in my law firm. Given the nature of the product, I determine that there is no residual value and the server system is likely to become completely obsolete with the passage of time. I anticipate that its useful life for my business will be approximately six years, so, using straight line depreciation, I will write off $833.33 per year over the course of six years in depreciation expense (that's an expense of $69.44 per month).

Now, let's change things around slightly and say that I anticipate being able to resell the server system for $1,000 after I've used it for six years. If this is the case, then I cannot depreciate the entire cost of the server, but only down to the salvage value. I subtract the $1,000 from the price paid to own the server, $5,000, and I get $4,000—this is the total amount that I'm allowed to depreciate, also known as the depreciable cost. I divide the $4000 by six years for a total of $666.67 in depreciation expense per year, or $55.56 per month.

Declining Balance Depreciation

Declining balance depreciation involves depreciating an asset by a greater amount early on in the asset's useful life and steadily depreciating less and less as time goes on. The assumption is that an asset depreciated using the declining balance method is going to lose more of its value in the earlier years of its usage. The mathematics here are fairly straightforward.

If you are going to use declining balance depreciation, you will first decide which rate to use; most commonly used are the 200 percent rate and the 150 percent rate. To offer you some perspective, straight line depreciation is at a 100 percent rate, meaning that if I need to depreciate $10,000 off of an asset with a useful life of ten years, then I divide 100 percent by ten years and I get 10 percent a year. So every year I depreciate 10 percent off of 10,000—that's $1,000 per year. I do this for ten years and I'm done. Now, using the same asset, let's say that we use declining balance depreciation at the 200 percent rate. We would divide 200 percent by 10 (years) to get 20 percent, and we would depreciate 20 percent off of the asset's *book value* every year. The "book value," in this case, is the value of an asset that is recorded by the company in its books. The book value declines as an asset is depreciated. If we depreciated $2,000 (20 percent) off of the $10,000 asset in year one, then the next year we would depreciate 20 percent off of the remaining book value of $8,000, and so forth.

Declining balance depreciation is not as commonly used as straight line depreciation. The essential idea of the declining balance method is that more value is written off earlier in the asset's life and less value is written off later.

Full Depreciation on Purchase

Did I say straight line depreciation was the simplest? I may have misspoken. Full depreciation on purchase may actually be the rightful claimant to that title.

Some assets depreciate so quickly that there is no need to depreciate them over a period of several years. You can just purchase them and write them off down to their salvage value. Computers and office furniture come to mind.

HANDS-ON LEARNING: For a more extensive review of depreciation methods with more real-world examples, please consider taking my online course.

Money Talks on the Statement of Cash Flows

From the assets section of PrintCo's balance sheet, we know that the company is currently sitting on about $1.9 billion in cash. An annual statement of cash flows may give a great deal of insight into how the company handles cash, particularly with regard to investments, financing activities, and dividend payouts.

As can be seen in the simplified statement of cash flows in figure 17, PrintCo's final cash position for the year (≈$1.9 billion) matches the value of the cash asset account on PrintCo's balance sheet for December 31. What else can we learn from this statement of cash flows?

Starting at the top, we will notice that, just as in Kathi's statement of cash flows, the incoming and outgoing cash flows from operating activities do not perfectly reflect the revenues and expenses detailed on PrintCo's income statement for the same period.

PrintCo
Statement of Cash Flows
For the Year Ending on 12/31/17 (all dollar amounts in millions)

Cash Flows from Operating Activities				
Cash flows from sales	$	8,627		
Outgoing cash from operating activities	$	(7,760)		
NET CASH FLOW FROM OPERATIONS			$	867
Cash Flows from Investing Activities				
New business purchase (net cash acquired)	$	(51)		
Property purchase	$	(96)		
Property sale	$	14		
Equipment purchase	$	(60)		
NET CASH FLOW FROM INVESTING			$	(193)
Cash Flows from Financing Activities				
Repurchase of common stock	$	(100)		
Dividends paid	$	(300)		
Issuance of notes payable	$	65		
NET CASH FLOW FROM FINANCING			$	(335)
Net Cash Flow			$	339
Cash position at the beginning of the period			$	1,585
Current cash position			$	1,924

GRAPHIC

fig. 17

REMEMBER

The income statements we have featured are built using accrual-based accounting methods. Cash flow statements do not directly track accrued revenue and expense but are informed instead by actual cash receipts.

NOTE

So-called "phantom expenses" such as depreciation—those that do not result directly in the outflow of cash—will show up as expenses on the income statement for several periods but will not affect the cash flow statement.

The cash flows from investing activities help recount some of the big moves that PrintCo made over the past year. They spent about $51 million buying out smaller businesses. "Net of cash acquired" means that the new cash assets acquired from the bought-out businesses reduced the total investment costs for the year to $51 million.

In the "cash flows from financing activities" section, we learn, among other things, that PrintCo decided to repurchase $100 million worth of its own common stock. Companies do this from time to time to signal confidence in the market and, hopefully, to get stock back out to the market at higher share prices, which translates into more incoming capital for the company.

These two specific activities, acquiring new businesses and buying back stock, are both indicative of a company that is in a favorable cash position, capable of making new, even somewhat speculative investments and pursuing new avenues for growth. The vitality of a company's cash position is often measured in terms of "free cash flow." **Free cash flow** can be defined as follows:

$$\begin{array}{ccccccc} \text{NET CASH FLOW} & & \text{CAPITAL} & & \text{CASH} & & \text{FREE} \\ \text{FROM OPERATIONS} & - & \text{EXPENDITURE} & - & \text{DIVIDENDS} & = & \text{CASH FLOW} \end{array}$$

The net cash flow from operations can be found on the bottom line in the first section of the statement of cash flows ($867 million in figure 17). Capital expenditures are investing activities related to expenditures on property, plant, or equipment, all items that are perceived to directly support the sustainability of a company's essential operations. Dividends are also included in this equation because companies are often under significant pressure to keep their dividend payments above certain thresholds. Simply put, capital expenditures and dividend payments are perceived to have "first dibs" on the cash generated by the company. Free cash flow is what is left over and available for more discretionary applications.

PrintCo's net cash provided by operating activities is $867 million. We can group "property purchase," "property sale," and "equipment purchase" (–96 + 14 + –60) to arrive at -$142 million in capital expenditure. Subtract our cash dividends (-300) from -142, and our free cash flow can be expressed as follows:

$867M – $442M = $425M

PrintCo has $425 million in cash that can be spent (or saved) with a high degree of flexibility. Companies with high free cash flow may wish to pay down longer-term debt, issue higher dividends, buy back stock, or make new investments or acquisitions.

In financial accounting, investors use the statement of cash flows to not only evaluate the strength of a company's cash position, but also to evaluate its vision for the future. Does the company seem more inclined to keep its investors happy through the issuing of reliable and generous dividend payments? Or is it more focused on investment and expansion?

From a managerial accounting perspective, the cash flow statement can be used to keep the business honest about its cash capabilities. Many business owners, including, presumably, several readers of this book, take an interest in accounting because their business has a bad habit of running out of cash. Perhaps the income statement looks healthy enough, but the bank accounts seem to persistently dwindle over time. By providing a space to track investment and financing activities, the statement of cash flows helps business owners and managers form a more complete picture of all business activities that generate and consume cash.

Chapter Recap

» Corporations with stockholders are more likely to use a retained earnings statement in place of a statement of owner's equity.

» The retained earnings statement documents the amount of net income remaining after a company pays out dividends to its stockholders.

» Multiyear income statements and earnings per share (EPS) are used to make intracompany comparisons, comparing the financial performance of a single company over successive time periods.

» Intercompany comparisons use ratios and other metrics to compare the financial performance of two or more different companies.

» "Current" assets and "current" liabilities imply an expectation that the asset will be liquidated (or the liability settled) within a year's time.

» Liquidity ratios evaluate a company's ability to meet its short-term obligations. Solvency ratios evaluate its ability to meet its obligations over the long term.

» Depreciation refers to incrementally writing off the expense of an investment over several successive periods.

» Free cash flow is the quantity of cash generated by net cash flow from business operations that is not confined to capital expenditures or dividend payments.

| 4 |
Assets = Liabilities + Equity

Chapter Overview
- » The Fundamental Accounting Equation
- » Intangible Assets
- » Debits and Credits
- » Loans and Amortization
- » Components of Equity
- » Corporate Equity

Double-entry bookkeeping was one hell of an invention.
— **CHARLIE MUNGER,** American Investor

Up to this point in our study, we have offered a fairly high-level view of accounting. Financial statements, in many ways, represent the finished product. But in order to craft any finished product, we first need to gather and process raw materials. In accounting, the raw materials are data, source documents, filing systems, rigorous data-entry protocols, journal entries, and other bookkeeping tools that must be properly applied and compiled if we are to produce accurate and actionable financial summary data (financial statements) for our business. In this chapter we are going to evacuate the hilltop and venture down into the trenches of accounting.

For you small business owners out there looking to harness the power of accounting to improve your business decision-making and organization, this chapter will prove incredibly useful (as will chapters 5, 6, 8, and 9).

Double-Entry Accounting
The title of this chapter is "Assets = Liabilities + Equities." You may recall this equation from chapter 1; it is known as the "fundamental accounting equation," it is reproduced on the balance sheet, and, for us accountants, it is the basis of everything we do, really!

The equilibrium between assets on one hand and liabilities plus equity on the other is maintained at all times by a critical accounting methodology known as "double-entry accounting." **Double-entry accounting** mandates that any change made to an account must be offset by a change to another account and that assets always remain equal to liabilities plus equity.

Double-entry accounting does *not* mean that every change to an account on the assets side of the fundamental accounting equation must be accompanied by a proportionate change on the liabilities/equity side.

If I purchased a $3,000 deli slicer for my meat-packing business, I would subtract the $3,000 from my cash (asset account). Then I would add $3,000 to my equipment account (also an asset account). The liability/equity side of the equation would not be affected.

In the preceding example, the cash account is technically being "credited" by $3,000 and the equipment account is being "debited" by $3,000. The strange but important concept of crediting and debiting in accounting will be explained later on in this chapter.

In other types of accounting entries, assets and liabilities/equity *are* adjusted simultaneously.

If I paid my employees a total of $7,500 on payday, I would subtract the $7,500 from my cash (asset account). Then, I would subtract $7,500 from my salaries and wages payable (liability account).

Notice how in the first example, with the deli slicer purchase, I *subtracted* from one asset account and *added* that amount to another asset account. In the payroll example, I *subtracted* from an asset account and *subtracted* that same amount from a liability account. The result of both transactions (and the result of all transactions) is that assets remain equal to liabilities plus equity.

We will be revisiting and applying double-entry accounting throughout this chapter and the rest of this book (and if you choose to become an accountant, you will likely be using double-entry accounting throughout your career). At the moment, though, let's take some time to understand more clearly how asset, liability, and equity accounts behave within the confines of double-entry accounting and within the fundamental accounting equation. As we do throughout this book, we will be utilizing the more formal and precise accrual basis accounting rather than cash basis accounting.

In cash basis accounting, a transaction is defined only by the movement of cash from one party to another. In accrual basis accounting, transactions are expressed in terms of accumulated assets and liabilities; that is, revenue and expenses are recorded as soon as (but not before) services are performed or goods are delivered, regardless of whether payment has been issued.

Assets

We briefly discussed asset accounts in chapter 1, within the context of a business's investment activities. When my meat-packing business invests in a new deli slicer, it acquires an asset. When my real estate company buys new property, it acquires an asset. But assets also include cash held in a checking account (or under the mattress). In accrual basis accounting, an asset can be an AR (accounts receivable) account—a record of what someone else owes your business.

Robbie's catering business agrees to provide catering for a wedding at a price of $6,400. The wedding was on May fifth, and Robbie's business provided catering but has yet to be paid. The $6,400 is added to Robbie's accounts receivable (asset account). When payment is received, the value of the business's AR account will be reduced, and the value of the business's cash account will be increased.

Think of asset accounts like AR as *forward-leaning*—they may be bereft of any intrinsic value for the moment, but they assert a promise of future value to come. The use of forward-leaning asset accounts, like accounts receivable, as well as forward-leaning liability accounts, like accounts payable, allows businesses to visualize their finances in a way that reflects actual real-time activities.

Intangible Assets

Patents, trademarks, copyrights, and trade names can be counted among a business's **intangible assets**. An intangible asset has no clearly defined immediate or even forward-leaning value. This does not mean, however, that intangible assets have no value whatsoever. Quite the contrary.

Nintendo may be one among many players in the fiercely competitive console-based gaming space, but the company sets itself apart with its robust catalog of highly sought-after intellectual property. Mario,

Zelda, Donkey Kong, and Pokemon (among others) would all be rightly considered intangible assets.

NOTE

In 2016 Nintendo valued its intangible assets at 9.98 billion Japanese yen (≈89.56 million US dollars).[7]

The pricing of intangible assets often has significant tax implications during the purchase or sale of a business.

Remember James, our PrintCo franchisee? Well, as it turns out, James's use of the PrintCo brand name for his shop did not come free of charge. In fact, a good chunk of the sales revenue reported on the PrintCo income statement from chapter 3 came from franchisees like James who were willing to pay good money for an intangible asset—the right to do business under the name "PrintCo." For accounting purposes, there are two ways in which James's deal with PrintCo is likely to be structured. First, PrintCo may ask James to pay an annual franchisee fee, let's say $5,000, for the right to use PrintCo branding, the benefit of PrintCo paid advertising, and all the other goodies that come with being a franchisee. James's accounting under this model would be very simple. He would record the annual $5,000 as an operating expense for tax and accounting purposes. The second, less likely, potential structuring of the franchisee deal would involve PrintCo asking James for a more substantial up-front payment in exchange for longer-term licensing of the PrintCo brand, let's say $45,000 for a ten-year license. In this case, rather than record as an operating expense the entire $45,000 in his first year of business, James will treat the acquisition of the license as an investment in an intangible asset. He (or his accountant) will create an intangible asset account called "franchise/licensing" valued at $45,000. From here, the intangible asset is treated in a manner similar to depreciable property. Every year James will record $4,500 ($45,000 divided by 10 years) in "amortization expense," and he will also deduct the accumulated amortization amount from the intangible asset account, "franchise/licensing." Assets, as always, will remain equal to the sum of liabilities and equity.

REMEMBER

Revenue and expense accounts are treated as equity accounts. See the Equity section of this chapter for further clarification. In the example above, James is deducting $4,500 in expenses (equity account) and also deducting $4,500 out of franchise/licensing (asset account). Hence, the equation remains balanced.

If a business purchases a machine and a ten-year franchise and sells them both the next year, then the value of both assets will have been diminished. Thus, amortization and depreciation are functionally the same thing. Simply put, property and equipment are depreciated; intangible assets are amortized.

Figure 18 shows what the assets section of James's balance sheet might look like after he had been a PrintCo franchisee for two years.

GRAPHIC

fig. 18

JAMES' PRINTCO FRANCHISE
Balance Sheet (Partial)
12/31/19

Assets				
Cash			$ 6,246	
Accounts receivable			$ 395	
Inventory			$ 2,100	
TOTAL CURRENT ASSETS				$ 8,741
Equipment	$ 2,570			
Less: Accumulated depreciation – equipment	$ 1,028	$ 1,542		
TOTAL PROPERTY, PLANT, EQUIPMENT				$ 1,542
Franchise/licensing	$ 45,000			
Less: Accumulated amortization – franchise/licensing	$ 9,000	$ 36,000		
TOTAL INTANGIBLE ASSETS				$ 36,000
TOTAL CURRENT ASSETS				$ 46,283

As detailed in figure 18, accumulated amortization is recorded on the balance sheet in the same way that property depreciation is recorded. After two years of being a franchisee, James has amortized a total of $9,000 worth of his franchising fee.

To be clear, when normal expenses are recorded—let's say James accumulates $500 in supplies expense and the supplies are purchased with cash—James's expense account (an equity account) will decrease and his cash (an asset account) will decrease to reflect the transaction. Assets will always be equal to liabilities plus equity. Pretty simple, right?

When an intangible asset—like a $45,000 ten-year license to use a major brand name—is first acquired (let's assume it was paid for with cash), the cash (asset account) will decrease by $45,000 and the franchise/licensing (asset account) will increase by $45,000, as with most any other major asset purchase. If James decides to amortize his intangible asset over a ten-year period, then every year he will decrease his expense (equity account) by $4,500 and decrease the value of the intangible asset by $4,500 to account for the amortization. Assets will remain (as always) equal to liabilities plus equity.

But wait, what if James didn't have $45,000 in cash lying around and took out a small business loan in order to get up and running with his PrintCo franchise? The issuance of the note (loan) would be recorded as follows: James (or his accountant) would increase his notes payable (liability account) by $45,000 and also increase his cash (asset account) by $45,000. Assets would continue to equal liabilities plus equity.

NOTE

If the entirety of the $45,000 in loan monies was going directly to pay for the licensing fee, then the transaction might be accounted for by simply increasing the notes payable (liability account) and immediately increasing the franchise/licensing (asset account).

QUESTION

Q: What if James, before opening his new business, already had $20,000 in cash that he was willing to put toward the $45,000 licensing fee, and he borrowed the remaining $25,000 from a lender? How might an accountant record the transaction?

Answer: The franchise/license (asset account) would be increased by $45,000. The cash account would be decreased by $20,000, and the loans payable account would be increased by $25,000. There would be a $25,000 net increase to the assets side of the balance sheet and a $25,000 increase to the liabilities/equity side. The intangible asset would be amortized just as it would have had James paid for it all with his own cash: the expense (equity account) would be decreased annually by $4,500, and the franchise/license (asset account) would be decreased through accumulated amortization by $4,500 each year.

Another type of intangible asset account commonly encountered by accountants is the patent. A *patent* constitutes an intangible asset because it gives companies a government-guaranteed exclusive right to manufacture and sell an invention. Like other intangible assets, patents are amortized over time. And, as with other intangible assets, the period of time over which the patent is amortized should reflect its expected usefulness. Patents often have legally mandated expiration dates. Prescription drugs, for example, cannot be indefinitely patented. In some industries, such as technology, the legal life of many patents will outlive their practical usefulness. If a software company patents a new antivirus program, for example, the patent may be legally enforceable for twenty years, but there is a good chance that within a ten-year window, competitors will find many other ways to effectively protect against viruses. Or perhaps the types of computers best served by the patented antivirus program will themselves become obsolete before the patent legally expires. Amortization periods for patents and other intangible assets should reflect the period of time during which the assets are expected to be useful. Let's walk through the process of acquiring and maintaining a patent on a new antivirus program, from an accountant's perspective.

» The patent for the new antivirus program is filed for and purchased— the total cost is $35,000, paid in cash. The cash (asset account) is decreased and the patent (asset account) is increased by $35,000.

» It is determined by the company that the patent will likely be useful for a period of seven years.

» After one year of holding the patent, the company decreases its expense (equity account) by $5,000 ($35,000/7) and decreases its patent (asset account) by $5,000 via accumulated amortization.

» Midway through the company's second year of holding the patent, a competitor challenges the validity of the patent in court. Though the patent is successfully defended, the company is forced to pay $10,000 in attorney and court fees (paid in cash). The cost of defending the patent, $10,000, is added to the patent (asset account). The company's cash (asset account) is reduced by $10,000.

» By the time the $10,000 is added to the patent (asset account), the patent has only five and a half years left of projected usefulness. The extra $10,000 will be amortized over the remaining ≈ five-year period: $2,000 in additional annual amortization is added to the $5,000 already being amortized for the patent.

» Each year for the next five years, the company reduces its expense (equity account) by $7,000 to account for amortization of the patent, and reduces the value of the patent (asset account) by $7,000 every year as well. Assets always remain equal to liabilities plus equity.

In the case of patents and other intangible assets, the initial value is always determined by the direct costs associated with producing the asset. For the patent, it would be attorney fees and filing fees. For an original piece of artwork, a cartoon character, or a logo, the value would be determined by factors such as the legal cost of the trademarking and the contract labor (graphic designers, artists, etc.).

But what happens when one intangible asset becomes clearly more valuable than another despite both having similar production costs?

Q: If Walt Disney paid an artist $50 to create Mickey Mouse and paid another artist $50 to create Walter Mouse (a character who never ended up getting used), how is it that both characters are valued at $50 despite one proving to be clearly more valuable than the other?

Answer: Intangible assets are valued according to their production costs until they are sold to another party. If Walt Disney sells all Mickey Mouse rights to Netflix to use and license out as they please, and Netflix pays $5 billion to secure these rights, then Netflix records the intangible asset of Mickey Mouse at the purchase price: $5 billion. Companies cannot simply mark up the value of their intangible assets on their balance sheets on the basis of their own estimations; there must be an actual sale.

Another frequently encountered example of an intangible asset is "goodwill." As the name implies, goodwill refers to the clearly valuable yet difficult-to-quantify assets associated with a company. Reputation is an example of goodwill. The value of a business's reputation may be due to its production of high-quality products, its competent and skilled staff, its high ethical standards, its strong community relations, or any variety of attributes.

Companies, of course, do not attempt to quantify the value of their own goodwill, as this would be inviting highly subjective valuations that would distort the reliability of financial statements. Instead, goodwill is quantified when companies buy out other businesses.

Brace yourself; the mechanics of acquiring goodwill for accounting purposes may seem a little strange at first.

Let's say that United Parcel Service, which already has about $3.8 billion worth of goodwill recorded on the assets section of its balance sheet,[8] decides to acquire a small trucking company called SuperFreight Inc. At the time of purchase, SuperFreight Inc. has $2.3 million in assets and $1.8 million in liabilities, a difference of half a million dollars. UPS agrees to pay $2 million in cash to acquire the company. SuperFreight Inc.'s assets are added to UPS's assets and its liabilities are added to UPS's liabilities. While the absorption of SuperFreight Inc. into UPS directly results in the acquisition of half a million more dollars' worth of assets than liabilities, UPS's payment of $2 million reduces its cash assets and leaves a net loss of $1.5 million in assets. The books will not be balanced!

Here is where goodwill comes in. Rather than allow companies to estimate their goodwill (bad idea), goodwill is calculated by finding the difference between the cost paid for acquiring a new business and the acquired business's assets minus their liabilities.

The difference between a company's assets and liabilities is known as "net asset value." It is what is left over if the company's assets are used to clear all of its liabilities.

Let's simplify this: UPS is paying $2 million to acquire (in its entirety) a company that has $2.3 million in assets and $1.8 million in liabilities (a net asset value of $0.5 million). If UPS pays $2 million to absorb this company into its own books, then its books are going to show a net decrease of $1.5 million in assets, a phenomenon that should never occur unless there is a proportionate decrease in UPS's liabilities or equity. To rectify the discrepancy *and* to quantify the intangible asset known as goodwill, the UPS accounting team will add $1.5 million to the goodwill (asset account). The books are now balanced; assets are equal to liabilities plus equity.

This more formal and standardized approach to quantifying goodwill is based on the idea that even though UPS paid more for SuperFreight Inc. than was warranted according to its net asset value, the fact that UPS is now able to plug SuperFreight's customer base, vehicles, and other valuables into the vast UPS infrastructure (a company with $3.8 billion in goodwill already accumulated)[9] makes the SuperFreight Inc. business more valuable now that it's in the hands of UPS. Make no mistake, UPS's $2 million dollar purchase price was not a charity offer. UPS was acting, presumably, to maximize its own interests and those of its stockholders. The fact that UPS found it viable to pay more than the acquired company's net asset value is a financial testament to its legitimate self-perception of the value of its own goodwill.

Goodwill is generally not amortized, because it is perceived to have perpetual, rather than finite, usefulness. It can, however, be downgraded. If a UPS driver runs over a small blind child, or if there is a massive labor strike due to accusations of unfair practices, then we have to account for the fact that the public relations fallout could have a substantial impact on the company's bottom line. In this event the company may choose to write down (reduce) the value of its goodwill (asset account). Loss of goodwill is considered an expense and shows up on the income statement. When the goodwill (asset account) is reduced, the expense (equity account) must be reduced by the same amount, keeping the equation in balance.

HANDS-ON LEARNING: More analyses, examples, and practice questions involving goodwill and other intangible assets can be found in my online course.

Liabilities

Liabilities represent value scheduled to depart the business. An example of a liability account is AP (accounts payable), money that you owe to another business or individual. Liabilities also include "notes payable" accounts, which are debts that your business is paying back to banks or other lenders (both short- and long-term debts). Liabilities include "unearned revenue" accounts, or services for which the business has already been paid but has yet to perform.

A self-employed and well-established professional rapper named E-Slice agrees to make a special guest appearance on the album of an up-and-comer in exchange for $100,000 in cash. The up-and-comer's record label pays E-Slice for the gig three weeks *before* the track is scheduled to be recorded. Even though E-Slice now has more value in his assets, $100,000 in cash, he also has an additional $100,000 in liabilities that will not go away until the work is performed, at which point the $100,000 will be moved from an unearned revenue account (liability account) to a normal revenue account (equity account).

Let's take a transaction-by-transaction accountant's view of what's happening in the preceding example.

After the deal is made and E-Slice gets paid, he adds $100,000 to his cash (asset account). E-Slice also records the $100,000 in an "unearned revenue" (liability account). Did I mention that E-Slice is also a student of accounting (one of his many hobbies) and that he's quite comfortable using simple spreadsheets for many of his self-managed accounting needs?

fig. 19

TRANSACTION RECORD	NOTE	DATE	ACCOUNT	**ASSETS**	**=**	ACCOUNT	**LIABILITIES**	**+**	ACCOUNT	**EQUITY**
1	Record Company Pays E-Slice	5/1/2018	Cash	$ 100,000		Unearned Revenue	$ 100,000		Revenue	$ -

Once E-Slice fulfills his obligation by recording the track, he decreases his unearned revenue (liability account) by $100,000 and increases his revenue (equity account) by $100,000.

fig. 20

TRANSACTION RECORD	NOTE	DATE	ACCOUNT	**ASSETS**	**=**	ACCOUNT	**LIABILITIES**	**+**	ACCOUNT	**EQUITY**
2	E-Slice Records the Track	6/1/2015	Cash	$ 100,000		Unearned Revenue	$ -		Revenue	$ 100,000

Unearned revenue, as shown in our example, operates similarly to notes payable. Notes payable accounts, however, are reduced by paying down debts, whereas unearned income accounts are reduced by delivering a good or performing a service. We mentioned notes payable in the Assets section of this chapter, when James had to take out a loan from the bank in order to partially fund his franchisee license. "Notes" refer to promissory notes, which can be issued by businesses to banks, suppliers—anyone, really. Since most lenders are not willing to lend money free of charge, notes payable liability accounts are often accompanied by interest payable accounts (which are also liability accounts). The cost of interest, like everything else, must be accounted for. But before we dive deeper into the intricacies of notes payable and interest payable, I believe the time has come to formally acquaint you with the central operating terms of double-entry accounting: debits and credits.

Debits & Credits

We have waited until near the midpoint of this chapter to introduce debits and credits. My hope was that you would first gain a basic sense of how double-entry accounting works (without having to worry about confusing terminology). If you have read this chapter straight through, then you probably understand the basic mechanics of double-entry accounting. If nothing else, you know that at least two things must transpire during any given accounting transaction:

1. When one account is adjusted, another account must be adjusted.
2. Assets must remain equal to the total of liabilities plus equity.

Up to this point, when we have described making changes to any given account, we have used the terms "increase" and/or "decrease." That is, when we pay a bill with cash we *decrease* our cash (asset account) by the amount of the bill and *decrease* our accounts payable (liability account) by the same amount. By replacing increase/decrease with debit/credit we will be introducing a more consistent and, once you get used to it, *less* confusing framework.

Every transaction in accounting involves both a debit and a credit. Take the simple accounts payable (AP) example just mentioned. Assume the amount of the bill being paid is $100. The cash (asset account) is credited $100 to reflect the decrease of cash, and the AP (liability account) is debited by $100 to reflect the decrease in the liability.

NOTE

The use of the terms "debit" and "credit" in accounting *does not* correspond to the normal usage of these terms by the general public. For example, when I return an item to a store, the store gives me "store credit," which I can spend on new merchandise. In accounting lingo, when asset accounts are increased, they are *debited*, and when asset accounts are reduced, they are *credited*. When I withdraw $100 from my checking account, I am technically crediting my checking account by $100. Crazy, right?

When a cash account (or any asset account) is credited, its value goes down. When a liability account is credited its value goes up.

When an accounts payable account or any liability account is debited, its value goes down. When an asset account is debited its value goes up.

EXAMPLE

A medical practice receives a cash payment of $150,000 from an insurance carrier. The practice's accountant debits the cash account by $150,000 and credits the accounts receivable (also an asset) account by the same amount.

EXAMPLE

An insurance company pays $150,000 to a medical practice to settle a claim for one of its customers. The insurance company's accountant credits the cash account by $150,000 and debits its accounts payable (liability account) by the same amount.

Simply put,

GRAPHIC

fig. 21

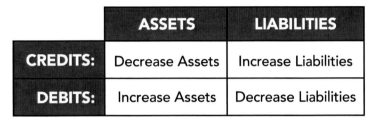

	ASSETS	**LIABILITIES**
CREDITS:	Decrease Assets	Increase Liabilities
DEBITS:	Increase Assets	Decrease Liabilities

NOTE

Equity accounts function very similarly to liabilities in terms of debits and credits, with a few slight nuances which we will review in the following section of this chapter.

Let's go back to the list from the beginning of this section regarding what must transpire during any given accounting transaction:

1. When one account is adjusted, another account must be adjusted.
2. Assets must remain equal to the total of liabilities plus equity.

Now let's add a third item:

3. Every transaction involves both a debit and a credit.

And a fourth item as well. This principle is also critical, but if you are brand new to accounting, it is going to take a little bit of practice before you can make good use of it:

4. Debits are always on the left and credits are always on the right.

If there ever was a cheerleading squad comprised entirely of accountants, this would be their go-to cheer:

> *Debits on the left! Credits on the right!*
> *Stand up, sit down,*
> *Fight! Fight! Fight! Fight!*

I remember this cheerleading chant from my days as an accounting student. I was fortunate to have very enthusiastic, high-spirited professors, the type that can really impact one's academic and professional development. (I believe I may already have mentioned Professor McFall; he is the original source for the debit/credit cheerleading chant).

GRAPHIC

fig. 22

ASSETS		=	LIABILITIES		+	EQUITY	
DEBIT	**CREDIT**		**DEBIT**	**CREDIT**		**DEBIT**	**CREDIT**
Increases asset value	Decreases asset value		Decreases liabilities *(value owed to others)*	Increases liabilities *(value owed to others)*		Decreases owner's capital	Increases owner's capital
						Decreases revenues	Increases revenues
						Increases expenses	Decreases expenses

In the fundamental accounting equation, assets are usually on the equation's left side and liabilities and equity are on its right. The normal situation in a business is a steady accumulation of assets. Property and real estate is acquired. Equipment is purchased. Money comes in and your checking account balances go up. Your assets should be somewhere in positive territory, pretty much all the time. Therefore, it is normal for your assets to have a "debit balance."

REMEMBER

Assets and debits are on the left. Assets have debit balances.

It is likewise normal for your liabilities (on the right side of the fundamental accounting equation) to have "credit balances." It is normal for a business to incur liabilities. So long as the business is ordering more new products to stock its inventories, the accounts payable liability account continues to increase. When customers make deposits (before goods have been shipped) the "customer deposits" liability account increases. Payable taxes are also a liability that should continually increase during the normal course of business.

REMEMBER

Liabilities and credits are on the right. Liabilities have credit balances.

If an asset or liability account has an abnormal balance—a credit balance in an asset account or a debit balance in a liability account—this is usually indicative of a record-keeping error. There are, of course, exceptions. If, for instance, the business overdraws its checking account, it will result in a credit balance.

Debits and credits are often denoted by the abbreviations "Dr." for debits and "Cr." for credits.

As you can see in figure 22, equity accounts are slightly more complex. We will go over the crediting and debiting of equity accounts later in this chapter.

Now that you have been given a primer on debits and credits, let's put our new, proper accounting terminology to work for us as we explore the rich and fascinating world of notes payable accounts.

Remember our self-employed professional rapper, E-Slice? Well, things have not gone so smoothly as of late with his record company. He is in the process of severing all ties and would like to start his own independent label, where he can not only release albums of his own but also promote new talent. He will need a financing source to get the ball rolling on this new endeavor.

Using his home as collateral, E-Slice finds a bank that will loan him the five million dollars he needs to get started. Once the financing is finalized, E-Slice debits his cash account by $5 million and credits his notes payable account.

TRANSACTION RECORD	NOTE	DATE	ACCOUNT	**ASSETS**	=	ACCOUNT	**LIABILITIES**	+	ACCOUNT	**EQUITY**
1	Financing	3/1/2019	Cash	$ 5,000,000		Notes Payable	$ 5,000,000		Revenue	$ -

fig. 23

The interest on E-Slice's loan accrues on a monthly basis at an annual rate of 6 percent. E-Slice makes his first payment after three months' time. Since interest accrues on the loan on a monthly basis, E-Slice has credited a liability account called interest payable every month for the last three months in the amount of $25,000 (.06 * 5,000,000 / 12).

TRANSACTION RECORD	NOTE	DATE	ACCOUNT	**ASSETS**	=	ACCOUNT	**LIABILITIES**	+	ACCOUNT	**EQUITY**
2	Accumulated Interest	4/1/2019		$ -		Interest Payable	$ 25,000		Expense	$ (25,000)
3		5/1/2019		$ -			$ 25,000			$ (25,000)
4		6/1/2019		$ -			$ 25,000			$ (25,000)

fig. 24

E-Slice Accrues $25,000 in Interest Expense Each Month

As you know, credits and debits come in pairs. When E-Slice's interest payable account was credited, another account had to be debited. Recall the main precept of accrual-based accounting: revenue is acquired and expenses are incurred on the basis of accrued obligation, not the transfer of cash. Even though E-Slice has not yet paid his first installment on the loan, he has already accrued interest liability (interest accrues every month) and can therefore report an interest expense.

Expense accounts are debited when expenses are incurred. Revenue accounts are credited when revenue is earned.

On June 15, E-Slice makes a payment of $107,741.62 on his loan.

fig. 25

TRANSACTION RECORD	NOTE	DATE	ACCOUNT	**ASSETS**	=	ACCOUNT	**LIABILITIES**	+	ACCOUNT	**EQUITY**
5	Loan Payment	6/15/2019	Cash	$ (107,741.62)		Interest Payable	$ (75,000.00)			
						Notes Payable	$ (32,741.62)			

When payment on the loan is made, the cash account is credited by $107,741.62, the interest payable account is debited by $75,000, and the notes payable account is debited by $32,741.62. From the $107,741.62 payment, $75,000 was used to pay off the accrued interest and $32,741.62 went toward the principal.

The structuring of a loan—interest rates, due dates, simple vs. compound interest, etc.—is detailed in an agreement between the lender and the borrower. The lender supplies an "amortization schedule," which details how much of each loan payment is applied toward interest and how much goes toward paying down the principal (figure 27). The accountant or bookkeeper uses the amortization schedule to record entries in a ledger. A good *bookkeeper*, using double-entry accounting, will be able to accurately record and organize all relevant transactions associated with the repayment of most any type of loan, whereas a good *accountant* will be able to both record transactions *and* intelligently advise the business on how various financing arrangements will impact overall financial strategy.

E-Slice will not make another payment until September. Meanwhile, interest continues to accumulate monthly at an annual rate of 6 percent. The loan principal was reduced slightly after the June payment, from $5,000,000.00 to $4,967,258.38. The 6 percent rate will be applied to the latter figure. Therefore, E-Slice's interest payable account will be credited $24,836.29 (.06 * $4,967,258.38 / 12) every month until his next payment.

fig. 26

TRANSACTION RECORD	NOTE	DATE	ACCOUNT	**ASSETS**	=	ACCOUNT	**LIABILITIES**	+	ACCOUNT	**EQUITY**
6	Accumulated Interest	7/15/2019		$ -		Interest Payable	$ 24,836.29		Expense	$ (24,836.29)
7		8/15/2019		$ -			$ 24,836.29			$ (24,836.29)
8		9/15/2019		$ -			$ 24,836.29			$ (24,836.29)
9	Loan Payment	9/15/2019		$ (107,741.62)			$ (74,508.87)			
						Notes Payable	$ (33,232.75)			

Notice how the 9/15 loan payment in the amount of $107,741.62 results in a $33,232.75 debit to the notes payable account, whereas the 6/15 payment of the same amount (figure 25) resulted in only a $32,741.62 debit to notes payable. Throughout the life of most loans, each successive payment becomes more heavily weighted toward paying down the principal (notes payable) rather than the interest (interest payable). As the principal goes down, less interest accumulates and more of the payment amount (which is usually fixed) can be applied to reducing the principal.

Figure 27 is an amortization schedule for E-Slice's loan through the year 2023. Notice how with each payment, less money is used to pay interest and more is applied to paying down the principal balance.

fig. 27

			AMORTIZATION SCHEDULE			
No.	Due Date	Payment	Additional Payment	Interest	Principal	Balance
						5,000,000.00
1	6/15/19	107,741.62		75,000.00	32,741.62	4,967,258.38
2	9/15/19	107,741.62		74,508.88	33,232.74	4,934,025.64
3	12/15/19	107,741.62		74,010.38	33,731.24	4,900,294.40
4	3/15/20	107,741.62		73,504.42	34,237.20	4,866,057.20
5	6/15/20	107,741.62		72,990.86	34,750.76	4,831,306.44
6	9/15/20	107,741.62		72,469.60	35,272.02	4,796,034.42
7	12/15/20	107,741.62		71,940.52	35,801.10	4,760,233.32
8	3/15/21	107,741.62		71,403.50	36,338.12	4,723,895.20
9	6/15/21	107,741.62		70,858.43	36,883.19	4,687,012.01
10	9/15/21	107,741.62		70,305.18	37,436.44	4,649,575.57
11	12/15/21	107,741.62		69,743.63	37,997.99	4,611,577.58
12	3/15/22	107,741.62		69,173.66	38,567.96	4,573,009.62
13	6/15/22	107,741.62		68,595.14	39,146.48	4,533,863.14
14	9/15/22	107,741.62		68,007.95	39,733.67	4,494,129.47
15	12/15/22	107,741.62		67,411.94	40,329.68	4,453,799.79
16	3/15/23	107,741.62		66,807.00	40,934.62	4,412,865.17
17	6/15/23	107,741.62		66,192.98	41,548.64	4,371,316.53
18	9/15/23	107,741.62		65,569.75	42,171.87	4,329,144.66
19	12/15/23	107,741.62		64,937.17	42,804.45	4,286,340.21

E-Slice's Amortization Schedule through 2023

As our transaction records make clear, only interest, not principal payments, are reported as expenses. You will see interest expense (along with all other expenses) on a company's income statement. Accumulated interest that has not yet been paid will show up on a business's balance sheet as "accrued interest."

Equity

A small tweak to the fundamental accounting equation will result in the following consubstantial expression:

$$\text{Assets} - \text{Liabilities} = \text{Equity}$$

And in this re-rendering of the formula we find the essence of equity: assets left over after a company's liabilities have all been settled. In the world of accounting, however, equity becomes a bit more complicated than simply figuring the value of a company's net assets. On our balance sheets we rely on equity accounts like "owner's equity" and "stockholder equity" to tell us who owns how much of the company's net assets. On our ledgers we not only track owner's equity and stockholder equity; we also use equity accounts to track our revenues and expenses.

Think of the expense account as the account that tracks the flow of money out of the business for normal operational upkeep. If I own a comic book shop (or any business), then I will certainly have expenses. I need to pay my rent. I need to pay my utilities. I need to pay my employees. I need to pay the interest on my business loan. All of this is money going out the door. This routine type of spending is different from purchasing a piece of equipment or a company car for my business. It's also different from buying inventory. When I spend money to purchase inventory or other assets, that's not "money out the door," because I have received in return assets of tangible value that theoretically can be resold. This spending is investment-related. Expenses, by contrast, relate not to the business's investment activities but to its operating activities. Paying my rent, my utilities, my employees, etc. are all operational expenses, the costs of doing business. Expenses reduce equity.

Now let's talk about revenue, the opposite of expense. When customers visit my store and my employees sell them products, I take in revenue. Think of revenue as money that flows into the business due to normal operational activity. Sales are revenue. Revenue increases equity.

Unpacking Equity in a Small Business

Sole proprietorships, partnerships, and LLCs do not have stockholders and therefore do not use stockholder equity accounts or dividends in their accounting.

The most common types of equity accounts used by these businesses include the following:

1. **Owner's capital balance / owner's equity** – used on the balance sheet, indicates owner's claim on company assets.

2. **Owner's contributions** – used on ledgers and on the statement of owner's equity, tracks money that the owner(s) puts into the business, increases owner's capital balance.

3. **Owner's withdrawals** – used on ledgers and on the statement of owner's equity, tracks money that the owner(s) takes out of the business, decreases owner's capital balance. Owner's withdrawals are, in a way, similar to dividend payments.

4. **Revenues** – appears on ledgers and on the income statement, tracks the increase in equity that transpires when the company takes in money, sometimes referred to as "sales," increases owner's capital balance.

5. **Expenses** – appears on ledgers and on the income statement, tracks the decrease in equity that occurs when the company depletes assets in the pursuit of additional revenues. Some examples are utilities expense, insurance expense, supplies expense, and payroll expense. Expenses decrease owner's capital balance.

Using our equity accounts, we can expand the fundamental accounting equation as follows:

Assets = Liabilities + (Owner's contributions – Owner's withdrawals + Revenue – Expenses)

As can be deduced from this expanded equation, equity is equal to owner's contributions – owner's withdrawals + revenue – expenses. And, in a small business, total equity is usually synonymous with the owner's capital balance that appears on the balance sheet.

NOTE

While you generally cannot have a negative asset balance (a credit balance) or a negative liability balance (a debit balance), it is certainly possible to have a negative equity balance (a debit balance). If total liabilities are greater than total assets, then the equity balance must be negative.

Equity is on the right side of the fundamental accounting equation; therefore, any actions that decrease equity are debits, and actions that increase equity are credits.

» When the owner's capital balance (equity) is increased, the transaction is a credit. When the owner's capital balance is decreased, the transaction is a debit.

» Owner's contributions are credits and owner's withdrawals are debits.

» When revenue increases (which always raises the owner's capital balance) it is considered a credit.

» When expenses increase (which always lowers the owner's capital balance) it is considered a debit.

The Ballad of Becky's Donut Shop

To illustrate small business accounting at work, we will now present The Ballad of Becky's Donut Shop.

Chapter (transaction) 1: Financing

Becky has finally saved up enough money to open her very own donut shop in downtown Louisville, Kentucky. As a sole proprietor, she does not need to submit any particular legal filings in order to go into business. All she needs are the requisite permits from the county and she will be selling delicious donuts in no time flat.

Becky is going to start her business using $100,000 of her own money. She opens a new business checking account and deposits her seed money.

You have been hired to be Becky's bookkeeper. Your first order of business is to debit Becky's cash account by $100,000 and credit her owner's contributions account by the same amount.

	ASSETS	=	LIABILITIES	+	OWNER'S EQUITY	
	Cash				Owner's Contributions	
(1)	$ 100,000				$ 100,000	

fig. 28

When an owner contributes money toward their business, they increase their equity in the business. All equity accounts are on the right; therefore, credits are used to record transactions that increase equity. Asset accounts are on the left; therefore, debits are used to record transactions that increase assets.

To track all of our adjustments to Becky's accounts, we are going to use a simple ledger on a spreadsheet. In the real world, most accountants and business owners input accounting data using software. The advantage of studying a ledger, regardless of how old-fashioned it may seem, is that it facilitates clearer insight into the logic of double-entry accounting.

Chapter (transaction) 2: Securing the Territory

Becky found a small building in a shopping center available for rent and thinks it will prove to be the perfect site for her new donut shop. She pays a refundable security deposit and her first month's rent. The deposit is $3,000 and rent is $1,500 a month.

As Becky's accountant, you must credit her cash account by $4,500 and debit her expense account by $1,500 to account for her first month's rent. The $3,000 security deposit is an asset, since it will presumably be returned to the business at some point in time. You therefore must create a "security deposits" account and make a $3,000 debit.

GRAPHIC

		ASSETS		=	LIABILITIES	+	OWNER'S EQUITY	
		Cash	Sec. Deposits				Owner's Contributions	Expense
(1)	$	100,000					$ 100,000	
(2)	$	(4,500)	$ 3,000					$ (1,500)
			Total Assets		Total Liabilities			Total Equity
		$	98,500		$ -		$	98,500

fig. 29

Because debits always lower total equity, when we record expense account "increases" (debits) or "increases" in an owner's withdrawal account (also debits), they are recorded as negative numbers. Similarly, when an asset account is lowered via a credit, the entry can be expressed as a negative number.

Chapter (transaction) 3: Gathering the Tools

In this chapter, Becky purchases the equipment she needs to make the donuts at her store. She invests in ovens, glazers, fryers, and some industrial-sized mixers. She pays for the equipment with cash, and her total expenditure is $25,000.

fig. 30

	ASSETS			=	LIABILITIES		+	OWNER'S EQUITY	
	Cash	Sec. Deposits	Equipment					Owner's Contributions	Expense
Previous Balances	$ 95,500	$ 3,000			$ -			$ 100,000	$ (1,500)
(3)	$ (25,000)		$ 25,000						
New Balances	$ 70,500	$ 3,000	$ 25,000					$ 100,000	$ (1,500)
			Total Assets			Total Liabilities			Total Equity
	$		98,500		$	-		$	98,500

Notice that in figure 30 the equipment purchase did not get recorded as an expense, but as an asset. Though relevant to the day-to-day operating activities of the business, the equipment purchase is an example of investing activity. Becky has *invested* in new assets for the business. The expense of these assets will be accounted for gradually, through depreciation. For example, we may decide to depreciate these new assets by $2,500 a year over the next ten years. Thus, each year we will credit the equipment (asset account) by $2,500 and debit the expense account by $2,500.

Expenses and revenues (not assets and liabilities) are what appear on a business's income statement and are used to measure profitability (and to assess tax obligations). Depreciation provides a method to fairly account for long-term investment costs.

Chapter (transaction) 4: Donuts Don't Make Themselves

Becky now has the equipment and the space she needs to make donuts. But in order to make donuts, you need actual dough. You also need powdered sugar, vanilla extract, and a bunch of different toppings and fillings. Becky wants these supplies coming in on a regular basis. In her search for a good wholesale vendor, she comes across Maverick's Food Supply. Maverick's has all the supplies she needs and then some, everything from premade Boston cream filling to paper napkins. Becky places her first order with Maverick's in the amount of $750. Maverick's fulfills the order on credit and promptly delivers the supplies. Becky won't have to pay until the end of the month.

fig. 31

	ASSETS			=	LIABILITIES		+	OWNER'S EQUITY	
	Cash	Sec. Deposits	Equipment		Accounts Payable			Owner's Contributions	Expense
Previous Balances	$ 70,500	$ 3,000	$ 25,000					$ 100,000	$ (1,500)
(4)					$ 750				$ (750)
New Balances	$ 70,500	$ 3,000	$ 25,000		$ 750			$ 100,000	$ (2,250)
			Total Assets			Total Liabilities			Total Equity
	$		98,500		$	750		$	97,750

Since the $750 worth of goods from Maverick's have been delivered, both the liability and the expense are recorded. The accounts payable (liability account) is credited in the amount of $750 and the expense (equity account) is debited by the same amount (see figure 31).

Maverick's is an AP, or accounts payable, account, which is used to track liabilities incurred when another business or person provides goods or services for which you have yet to pay. All AP accounts are liabilities, as they indicate a future obligation.

If we wanted to be extremely formal in our treatment of Becky's accounting ledger, we would debit her asset account by $750 rather than debiting her expense account. The $750 would go into an "inventory" asset account, and as the materials were used up and donuts were sold to customers, we would steadily credit the inventory account to reflect the diminishment of the inventory, and we would steadily debit a "cost of goods sold" (expense account), tracking all expenses directly stemming from inventory costs. The "value" of this cost of goods sold expense account would then be reported on the business's income statement at the end of the period.

Simply put, were we to use more formal inventory accounting, the price of the donut-making material purchased from Maverick's would not immediately go into Becky's expense account as soon as the material was delivered. It would first be held in an inventory (asset account) and would only go into the expense account after it was sold to customers. For a more thorough discussion on the treatment of inventory in accounting, please see the Accounting for Inventory section in chapter 6.

For a small donut shop, accounting for the precise inflow and outflow of inventory would prove quite tedious, especially if we continue to assume that the donuts are being made fresh on-site. Our simplified method, as shown in figure 31, of moving all raw donut-making materials immediately into expenses is most likely appropriate for a business of this nature.

Were Becky retailing merchandise with more substantial and clearly defined wholesale costs, such as surf boards, computers, books, or shoes, then it might make more sense for her to use an inventory asset account and a cost of goods sold expense account to track the flow of inventory through the business. When businesses are holding too much of their assets in inventory, they are more vulnerable to cash flow problems. When they hold too little in inventory, they are in danger of losing sales and frustrating their customers. For a donut shop, however, most "inventory" will not be held much longer than 24 hours. It will be disposed of regularly (and, using formal methods, disposed-of inventory would also have to be credited out of inventory and debited into expenses, another extra and likely unnecessary step). Profit margins in donut shops are known to be high; the cost required to make a donut should be much less than the retail price of the donut. Becky should not have to worry about inventory expense eating too deeply into her revenues. Furthermore, under normal circumstances Becky will not be returning donut-making materials to Maverick's or any other supplier. Some materials that are purchased will inevitably end up wasted, and that is to be expected. But rather than go to the trouble of treating donut-making materials as assets, we can provide Becky with sound bookkeeping by simply treating these materials as expenses and debiting them out of our equity upon receipt, as is shown in figure 31.

When the goods are paid for at the end of the month, the accounts payable account (liability) will be debited by $750 and the cash account (asset) will be credited by the same amount.

Chapters (transactions) 5 & 6: Finding Good Help and Opening Up

for Business

Becky anticipates that when she first opens up she will be met by a rush of customers wanting to try out the new donut shop. In anticipation, she decides to hire two employees before opening day.

After week one is in the books, Becky's Donut Shop has recorded $4,235 in sales. Her two employees have worked a combined sixty-three hours, and she has agreed to pay them each $10 per hour, though paychecks won't go out until the end of week two.

fig. 32

	ASSETS			=	LIABILITIES		+	OWNER'S EQUITY		
	Cash	Sec. Deposits	Equipment		Accounts Payable	Accrued Payroll		Owner's Contributions	Expense	Revenue
Previous Balances	$ 70,500	$ 3,000	$ 25,000		$ 750			$ 100,000	$ (2,250)	$ -
(5) (6)	$ 4,235					$ 630			$ (630)	$ 4,235
New Balances	$ 74,735	$ 3,000	$ 25,000		$ 750	$ 630		$ 100,000	$ (2,880)	$ 4,235
			Total Assets			Total Liabilities				Total Equity
	$		102,735		$	1,380		$		101,355

The $4,235 in sales is recorded by debiting cash and crediting revenue (transaction 5), and the $630 accrued payroll expense is recorded by crediting an accrued payroll liability account and debiting the expense account.

Our treatment of accrued payroll expenses in this example is simplified and does not include payroll taxes such as unemployment taxes, workers compensation insurance, and the employer's share of FICA (Social Security and Medicare). Accountants usually add in these additional costs to their accrued payroll ledger entries.

As you can see in figure 32, the revenue collected from the week is recorded both in the revenue equity account and the cash asset account. When you (Becky's accountant) help Becky assess her finances at the end of her first week of business, you'll presumably have all of the cash from her revenue on hand and will be able to immediately deposit it into her bank account, or wherever she stores her cash assets. With payroll, however, although you have recorded the liability and the expense, it does not affect the cash supply at this time. Becky's employees won't be paid until the following week. However, since the services of the employees have already been rendered, the obligation becomes what is known as an accrued liability and must be debited out of your equity. As you may have noticed, we have made two separate transaction records: the collection of revenue and a record of accrued employee payroll liability.

Chapters (transactions) 7, 8, 9 & 10: Grease Fire

Everything is going swimmingly at Becky's Donut Shop until an unattended fryer suddenly bursts into flame. A vicious grease fire breaks out and persists for several seconds before one of Becky's employees extinguishes it. The fire does significant damage to the walls and the ceiling.

Becky's landlord comes to survey the damage, bringing along one of his contractors. The contractor estimates that replacing the damaged ceiling area and the drywall, plus the repainting, is going to cost $3,500. He won't be free to do the work until the following week. Becky's landlord offers to use Becky's $3,000 security deposit to help pay for the damage. Becky will pay for the remaining $500 out-of-pocket. Becky and her landlord decide to immediately pay the contractor his estimated $3,500, so he can purchase the materials he needs to do the job next week.

Meanwhile, despite the accident, Becky does $3,910 worth of sales in week two, a decline of about 8 percent from the previous week. Her two employees work a combined sixty-nine hours during week two, accumulating $690 in wages, all of which, in addition to the wages from week one (a total of $1,320) are paid at the end of week two.

fig. 33

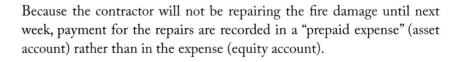

	ASSETS				=	LIABILITIES		+	OWNER'S EQUITY		
	Cash	Sec. Deposits	Prepaid Exp.	Equip.		Accounts Payable	Accrued Payroll		Owner's Contributions	Expense	Revenue
Previous Balances	$ 74,735	$ 3,000		$ 25,000		$ 750	$ 630		$ 100,000	$ (2,880)	$ 4,235
(7)	$ (500)	$ (3,000)	$ 3,500								
(8)(9)	$ 3,910						$ 690			$ (690)	$ 3,910
(10)	$ (1,320)						$ (1,320)				
New Balances	$ 76,825	$ -	$ 3,500	$ 25,000		$ 750	$ -		$ 100,000	$ (3,570)	$ 8,145
			Total Assets			**Total Liabilities**				**Total Equity**	
	$			105,325		$	750		$		104,575

Because the contractor will not be repairing the fire damage until next week, payment for the repairs are recorded in a "prepaid expense" (asset account) rather than in the expense (equity account).

In accrual-based accounting, expenses are debited out of equity when services are performed or when goods switch hands, regardless of when payment is made.

Chapters (transactions) 11, 12, 13, 14, 15, 16, 17: Repairs and Pet Matters

A day into week three at the donut shop, the big fryer, the one that caught on fire last week, does not seem to be working properly. The fryer was visibly damaged by the fire. With a call to the manufacturer, Becky learns that any fire damage is sufficient to void the warranty. If there is any hope of getting this $2,000 piece of equipment back in action, Becky is going to have to deal with it herself and foot the bill.

The repairman comes in on Wednesday and fixes the problem. The cost of parts and labor for the repair come to $276, which is definitely preferable to spending $2,000 for a full replacement. The repairman does not collect his payment right away but says he will send Becky a bill.

The fire damage on the wall and ceiling are repaired by the landlord's contractor on Friday. Materials and labor end up at $3,350, which is $150 less than the original estimate. Since the contractor has already been paid $3,500, he returns $150 to Becky.

The revenue from week three is $4,690 and the accrued payroll expense is $720, but the employees won't be paid until the following week. Also, Becky pays her first bill from Maverick's, $750, and she receives her second major shipment of baking materials and supplies, an order worth $1,030.

Meanwhile, there is a personal matter at hand. TumblerBun, Becky's 15-year-old cat, requires a very expensive surgery, and Becky has decided to take $3,200 in cash out of the business in order to pay for it.

fig. 34

	ASSETS			=	LIABILITIES		+	OWNER'S EQUITY			
	Cash	Prepaid Exp.	Equipment		Accounts Payable	Accrued Payroll		Owner's Contrib.	Owner's Withdr.	Expense	Revenue
Previous Balances	$ 76,825	$ 3,500	$ 25,000		$ 750	$ -		$ 100,000		$ (3,570)	$ 8,145
(11)					$ 276					$ (276)	
(12)	$	150	$ (3,500)							$ (3,350)	
(13)(14)	$ 4,690					$ 720				$ (720)	$ 4,690
(15)	$ (750)				$ (750)						
(16)(17)	$ (3,200)				$ 1,030				$ (3,200)	$ (1,030)	
New Balances	$ 77,715	$ -	$ 25,000		$ 1,306	$ 720		$ 100,000	$ (3,200)	$ (8,946)	$ 12,835
			Total Assets			**Total Liabilities**					**Total Equity**
	$		102,715		$	2,026		$			100,689

Becky certainly has a lot going on this week and there is definitely a chance that a mistake or two might be made in the books. You can always double-check the validity of your accounting by testing whether or not total assets are equal to total liabilities plus total equity. If the equation is not equal, then there must be some error in the bookkeeping.

Let's say, for instance, that we were off by $150—our assets were $150 less than the sum of our liabilities and equity. Instead of looking like the ledger depicted in figure 34, our ledger included a small error and looked something like this:

fig. 35

	ASSETS			=	LIABILITIES		+	OWNER'S EQUITY			
	Cash	Prepaid Exp.	Equipment		Accounts Payable	Accrued Payroll		Owner's Contrib.	Owner's Withdr.	Expense	Revenue
Previous Balances	$ 76,825	$ 3,500	$ 25,000		$ 750	$ -		$ 100,000		$ (3,570)	$ 8,145
(11)					$ 276					$ (276)	
(12)		$ (3,500)								$ (3,350)	
(13)(14)	$ 4,690					$ 720				$ (720)	$ 4,690
(15)	$ (750)				$ (750)						
(16)(17)	$ (3,200)				$ 1,030				$ (3,200)	$ (1,030)	
New Balances	$ 77,565	$ -	$ 25,000		$ 1,306	$ 720		$ 100,000	$ (3,200)	$ (8,946)	$ 12,835
			Total Assets			**Total Liabilities**					**Total Equity**
	$		102,565		$	2,026		$			100,689

Notice that in figure 35 total assets are equal to $102,565, which is $150 less than the sum of total liabilities and total equity. However, if we look at our "previous balances" in figure 35, we can see that our equation was perfectly balanced, with $105,325 on each side. We have an error in one or more of our transactions 11-17. Since our error amount is $150 and is missing on the assets side, a good first step is to look for any $150 credit that does not have a corresponding debit.

Unfortunately, there is neither a credit nor a debit for $150 in figure 35. We will need to go through each transaction and verify that the amount debited was equal to the amount credited. In transaction 12, we have a $3,500 asset credit corresponding to a $3,350 expense debit, a difference of $150. If we go back to the source material for the transaction, we will find a paid invoice in the amount of $3,350 for the repair of the wall and the ceiling. The invoice should also notate that $150 was returned to the customer to refund the overage from a $3,500 prepayment. That $150 should have either been recorded as a debit to the cash account (as it was in figure 34)—assuming it ended up in the cash register and eventually found its way into the company checking account—or it might be a debit to the owner's withdrawal equity account if Becky put the refunded amount from the contractor directly into her purse. In any event, the missing $150 needs to be debited somewhere.

In this example, we discovered the accounting error when we noticed that assets were not equal to liabilities plus equity. A more commonly noticed red flag is when the business's cash account does not properly reconcile with the actual cash balance reported on its bank statement. For instance, if the $150 had been put in the cash register, then the actual bank statement balance would end up being $77,715, or $150 more than the $77,565 new cash balance shown on the accounting ledger in figure 35. We would have known right out of the gate that we were looking for a cash discrepancy, specifically a missing cash debit, and that may have helped us zero in more quickly on the error.

Epilogue: End-of-Period Financial Statements for Becky's Donut Shop

On her way to take TumblerBun to the veterinarian, Becky asks us to prepare an income statement, balance sheet, and cash flow statement for her donut shop. Using the information recorded on our ledgers we can easily produce these basic statements. In fact, you might want to take a shot at it on your own before reading the following walk-through:

The first step is to take an inventory of Becky's current accounts and their values (figure 36).

The first financial statement we will create for Becky is her income statement, which, if you recall from chapter 2, focuses on the total revenues over total expenses. Becky's revenues have come exclusively from sales thus far. Her expenses, however, have been more diverse. We will want to take a moment to differentiate the components of our total $8,946 worth of expenses that have been racked up over the last few weeks (figure 37).

fig. 36

ASSET ACCOUNTS		VALUE
Cash	$	77,715.00
Equipment	$	25,000.00
LIABILITY ACCOUNTS		
Accounts Payable	$	1,306.00
Accrued Payroll	$	720.00
OWNER'S EQUITY ACCOUNTS		
Owner's Contributions	$	100,000.00
Owner's Withdrawals	$	(3,200).00
Expense	$	(8,946).00
Revenue	$	12,835.00

fig. 37

EXPENSES		VALUE
Rent	$	1,500.00
Materials	$	1,780.00
Payroll	$	2,040.00
Maintenance and Repairs	$	3,626.00

After going through our ledgers, we can identify four different expense types: rent, materials, payroll, and repairs/maintenance. In accounting, each of these different expense types is referred to as a separate expense "account." Had we been keeping a more formal ledger, we would have given a separate column to each expense account in play. The combined total value of all of Becky's identified expenses is $8,946, which matches the new balance recorded at the end of our last ledger entry.

fig. 38

	ASSETS			=	LIABILITIES		+	OWNER'S EQUITY			
	Cash	Prepaid Exp.	Equipment		Accounts Payable	Accrued Payroll		Owner's Contrib.	Owner's Withdr.	Expense	Revenue
Previous Balances	$ 76,825	$ 3,500	$ 25,000		$ 750	$ -		$ 100,000		$ (3,570)	$ 8,145
(11)					$ 276					$ (276)	
(12)	$ 150	$ (3,500)								$ (3,350)	
(13)(14)	$ 4,690					$ 720				$ (720)	$ 4,690
(15)	$ (750)				$ (750)						
(16)(17)	$ (3,200)				$ 1,030				$ (3,200)	$ (1,030)	
New Balances	$ 77,715	$ -	$ 25,000		$ 1,306	$ 720		$ 100,000	$ (3,200)	$ (8,946)	$ 12,835
			Total Assets			**Total Liabilities**					**Total Equity**
	$		102,715		$	2,026		$			100,689

And here is our income statement (figure 39):

Becky's Donut Shop
Income Statement
For the Month Ending on 8/31/18

Revenues			
Sales revenue	$	12,835	
TOTAL REVENUES		$	12,835
Expenses			
Rent expense	$	1,500	
Materials expense	$	1,780	
Payroll expense	$	2,040	
Maintenance and repairs expense	$	3,626	
TOTAL EXPENSES		$	8,946
Net income		$	3,889

For the purpose of this example, we are going to assume that all of the events described in our ledger transpired during the month of August in the year 2018.

Income statements, statements of owner's equity, and cash flow statements reflect a particular *period* of time, usually a month, a quarter, or a year. Balance sheets reflect the financial realities of a particular *moment* in time.

Next, we are going to create a statement of owner's equity and a balance sheet:

Becky's Donut Shop
Statement of Owner's Equity
For the Month Ending on 8/31/18

OWNER'S EQUITY ON 7/31/18		$	-
Owner's contributions	$	100,000	
Owner's withdrawals	$	(3,200)	
Net income for the month	$	3,889	
TOTAL	$	100,689	
OWNER'S EQUITY ON 8/31/18		$	100,689

Becky's Donut Shop
Balance Sheet
8/31/18

Assets			
Cash		$	77,715
Equipment		$	25,000
TOTAL ASSETS		$	102,715

Liabilities and Equity					
Liabilities					
	Accounts payable	$	1,306		
	Accrued payroll	$	720		
	TOTAL LIABILITIES			$	2,026
Equity					
	Becky Robinson, contributions	$	100,000		
	Becky Robinson, withdrawals	$	(3,200)		
	Current revenue	$	3,889		
	TOTAL EQUITY			$	100,689
TOTAL LIABILITIES PLUS TOTAL EQUITY				$	102,715

GRAPHIC

fig. 41

One of the nice things about being a sole proprietor is that your business's total equity value is synonymous with your ownership claim. The figure 41 balance sheet tells us that Becky, in large part because of her sizable $100,000 contribution in seed money to start her business, has a sizable claim on the business's assets, with liabilities (debts) of only $2,026. Imagine how different her balance sheet might look had she taken out a bank loan for $100,000 rather than using her own money. Perhaps something like figure 42.

In the figure 42 balance sheet, it is the business's creditors, namely the owner of the note payable, who exerts the greatest claim on the company's assets. The business owner, Becky, would build more equity in the business by consistently turning profits and by paying down the note.

Creating a statement of cash flows for Becky's Donut Shop would typically involve a review of the business's receipts or checking account ledger, documenting cash departing or arriving in the business. Cash flows are the result of either an operating activity, an investing activity, or a financing activity.

Becky's Donut Shop
Balance Sheet
8/31/18

fig. 42

Assets		
Cash	$	77,715
Equipment	$	25,000
TOTAL ASSETS	$	102,715

Liabilities and Equity				
Liabilities				
Accounts payable	$	1,306		
Notes payable	$	100,000		
Accrued payroll	$	720		
TOTAL LIABILITIES			$	102,026
Equity				
Becky Robinson, contributions	$	-		
Becky Robinson, withdrawals	$	(3,200)		
Current revenue	$	3,889		
TOTAL EQUITY			$	689
TOTAL LIABILITIES PLUS TOTAL EQUITY			$	102,715

Let's look at the first recorded cash flow on our ledger. After Becky contributed $100,000 to open the business, we made a debit entry of $100,000 to the business's cash account. In our statement of cash flows, this movement of cash will be categorized as a financing activity. We have to be careful, though, because some single cash transactions may be relevant to multiple types of business activity. In our second ledger entry, when Becky paid $4,500 to the owner of the leasing space, $1,500 went to pay for the first month's rent while $3,000 went to the security deposit, an asset account. The $1,500 is categorized as outgoing cash for operational activities, and the $3,000 would be categorized under investing activities. After reviewing and categorizing all cash flows for the period, our statement of cash flows for Becky's Donut Shop might look something like figure 43.

After identifying and categorizing all of our cash flows, we can check our "current cash position" against our cash asset value as it appears on the balance sheet. Both are $77,715. While the creation of Becky's cash flow statement was straightforward for the most part, there were a couple of areas where things got a little tricky. For starters, when calculating the outgoing cash from operating activities, you are basically looking for business expenditures that resulted in both a debit to the expense account and a credit to the cash account within the specified statement period. These two transactions *do not* necessarily have to take place at the same time. The first cash payment to Maverick's (transaction 15) of $750 dollars took place after the $750 expense was incurred (transaction 4).

fig. 43

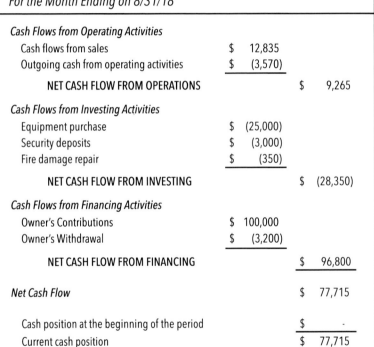

Becky's Donut Shop
Statement of Cash Flows
For the Month Ending on 8/31/18

Cash Flows from Operating Activities		
Cash flows from sales	$ 12,835	
Outgoing cash from operating activities	$ (3,570)	
NET CASH FLOW FROM OPERATIONS		$ 9,265
Cash Flows from Investing Activities		
Equipment purchase	$ (25,000)	
Security deposits	$ (3,000)	
Fire damage repair	$ (350)	
NET CASH FLOW FROM INVESTING		$ (28,350)
Cash Flows from Financing Activities		
Owner's Contributions	$ 100,000	
Owner's Withdrawal	$ (3,200)	
NET CASH FLOW FROM FINANCING		$ 96,800
Net Cash Flow		$ 77,715
Cash position at the beginning of the period		$ -
Current cash position		$ 77,715

Another difficulty encountered when creating this particular statement of cash flows was tracking the real impact of the grease fire on the business's cash supply. To repair the damage caused by the fire, a prepayment was made to a contractor (transaction 7) of $3,500—$3,000 coming from the security deposit (asset account) and $500 coming from the business's cash account—but only $3,350 was ultimately used to make repairs, and $150 was returned to the cash account. Since the $3,000 security deposit cash outflow had already been accounted for on the cash flow statement, we took the difference between $500 and $150 to arrive at a net $350 outflow of cash for fire damage repair.

Unpacking Equity in a Corporation

If you have been able to follow the use of double-entry accounting in Becky's Donut Shop, then you should also be able to follow the double-entry accounting used by a Fortune 500 company. At the end of the day, numbers are numbers. Some are just bigger than others.

Before you go charging in headfirst, though, you need to understand how equity is structured within a corporation.

fig. 44

ASSETS = LIABILITIES + STOCKHOLDERS' EQUITY

COMMON STOCK + RETAINED EARNINGS

REVENUES − EXPENSES − DIVIDENDS

Corporations are owned entirely by stockholders, who supply the corporation with capital and receive common stock shares and dividends in return. When accounting for corporations, the issuing of common stock is analogous to an owner's contribution. If a company issues a million dollars' worth of common stock, then the cash (asset account) is debited by a million and the common stock (equity account) is credited by a million.

NOTE

Stock issues are "common stock" unless otherwise specified. Common stockholders have voting rights and stand to profit greatly when the company succeeds. About 6 percent of companies in the US also issue "preferred stock," which offers investors more stable dividend payments but is not necessarily, as the name might imply, a superior investment. If a company issues preferred stock, then the equity held by preferred stockholders is accounted for by way of a separate, preferred stock equity account.

The retained earnings of a corporation, as was discussed in chapter 2, are essentially net income minus dividend payments. Retained earnings are the profit that the company keeps for itself for investment, expansion, and operational upkeep. Retained earnings is a standard right-side account—on the right side of the fundamental accounting equation—and therefore, increases to retained earnings are credits and decreases to retained earnings are debits.

Dividends operate similarly to expenses in that they reduce stockholder equity when increased. When a corporation pays out a dividend to shareholders, the dividend (equity account) is debited and the cash (asset account) is usually credited. I say "usually" because although most dividend payouts are cash payouts, it is possible for dividends to be issued in forms other than cash. A debit balance is the normal balance for a dividend account. The common stock (equity account) increases in value when it is credited and decreases in value when it is debited. A credit balance is a normal balance for common stock.

An easy way to remember how all equity accounts behave in relation to credits and debits is to think of anything that lowers stockholder equity (such as increases in expenses and increases in dividends) as being a debit, whereas anything that raises stockholder equity, such as increases in revenue or increases in common stock, are credits.

The normal balance for an asset account is a debit balance, and the normal balance for a liability account is a credit balance. The equity account, as a whole, should have a credit balance in normal circumstances. Expenses and dividends, however, although they are technically equity accounts, actually reduce equity value. Expenses and dividends have debit balances under normal conditions.

fig. 45

ASSETS = LIABILITIES + STOCKHOLDERS' EQUITY

↑ DEBITS   ↑ CREDITS   ↑ CREDITS ↓ DEBITS
↓ CREDITS   ↓ DEBITS

COMMON STOCK + REVENUES − EXPENSES − DIVIDENDS

↑ CREDITS   ↑ CREDITS ↑ DEBITS ↑ DEBITS
↓ DEBITS   ↓ DEBITS ↓ CREDITS ↓ CREDITS

Retained earnings (revenues − expenses − dividends), as a whole, increase stockholder equity. If a corporation's revenue is $100M, its expenses are $90M, and it returns $3M in dividends back to stockholders, then the $7M in retained earnings serves to increase the stockholders' claims on company assets. This is the same principle as when a small business turns a profit (revenues exceed expenses); that profit boosts the owners' equity value in the business. Remember, cash that comes into a business via financing activities often belongs to creditors. The creditors have a claim that entitles them to repayment. Cash that comes into the business by way of operating activities (revenues) belongs to the business's (or corporation's) owners (stockholders). The owners/stockholders may need to use some or all of that cash to service loans and other liabilities. Nevertheless, profits/net income/retained earnings always contribute to a net increase in owner/stockholder equity.

Imagine a corporation (Corporation X) financed through the issuing of $10M in common stock and $7M in loans.

* ALL NUMBERS IN THOUSANDS	ASSETS	=	LIABILITIES	+	STOCKHOLDER'S EQUITY			
	Cash		Notes Payable		Common Stock	Revenue	Expenses	Dividends
(1) (2)	$ 17,000		$ 7,000		$ 10,000			

** ALL NUMBERS IN THOUSANDS **

fig. 46

After one full quarter of operations, the following financial events have transpired:

	ASSETS			=	LIABILITIES		+	STOCKHOLDER'S EQUITY			
	Cash	Other Assets	Accts. Rec.		Notes Payable	Accts. Payable		Common Stock	Revenue	Expenses	Dividends
(1) (2)	$ 17,000				$ 7,000			$ 10,000			
Previous Balances	$ 17,000				$ 7,000			$ 10,000			
(3)	$ (100)				$ (100)						
(4)	$ (12,000)	$ 12,000									
(5)	$ 2,563		$ 2,000						$ 4,563		
(6)	$ (2,055)					$ 1,000				$ (3,055)	
(7)	$ (500)										$ (500)
New Balances	$ 4,908	$ 12,000	$ 2,000	$	6,900	$ 1,000	$	10,000	$ 4,563	$ (3,055)	$ (500)
			Total Assets			Total Liabilities					Total Stockholder Equity
	$		18,908	$		7,900	$				11,008

** ALL NUMBERS IN THOUSANDS **

fig. 47

(1) $10,000,000 in common stock is issued.
   Debit Cash / Credit Common Stock

(2) $7,000,000 in business loans is procured.
   Debit Cash / Credit Notes Payable

(3) A $100,000 payment is made to pay down loans.
   Debit Notes Payable / Credit Cash

(4) Corporation X purchases $12,000,000 worth of equipment and supplies.
   Debit Other Assets / Credit Cash

(5) Corporation X earns $4,563,000 in revenues; $2,563,000 is received in cash and the rest is owed.
   Debit Cash and Accounts Receivable / Credit Revenue

(6) Corporation X incurs $3,055,000 worth of expenses; $2,055,000 is paid in cash and the rest is owed.
Debit Expenses / Credit Cash and Accounts Payable

(7) Corporation X issues a $500,000 dividend payment to its stockholders.
Debit Dividends / Credit Cash

NOTE

Figure 47 depicts a highly generalized ledger. For a more granular view of day-by-day accounting, please refer to the previous section in this chapter, The Ballad of Becky's Donut Shop.

Corporation X's first quarter financial data shows $4,563,000 in total revenue and $3,055,000 in total expenses. The corporation's income statement would thus show a net income of $1,508,000.

Corporation X issues a dividend payment to its investors in the amount of $500,000. From here we can calculate retained earnings at $1,008,000.

fig. 48

Corporation X **Retained Earnings Statement** *End of Quarter (all dollar amounts in thousands)*		
Retained Earnings at the beginning of the period	$	-
Plus: Net income	$	1,508
	$	1,508
Less: Dividends issued	$	500
Retained Earnings at the end of the period	$	1,008

Retained earnings (along with common stock) will show up in the equity section of Corporation X's balance sheet (figure 49).

Retained earnings are added back into the stockholders' equity total.

REMEMBER

The essential difference between common stock and retained earnings is that common stock is capital provided by stockholder investments, and retained earnings is capital provided by the company's own business operations.

Corporation X
Balance Sheet
End of Quarter (all dollar amounts in thousands)

Assets

Cash	$	4,908
Accounts receivable	$	2,000
Other Assets	$	12,000
TOTAL ASSETS	$	18,908

Liabilities and Equity

Liabilities

Accounts payable	$	1,000		
Notes Payable	$	6,900		
TOTAL LIABILITIES			$	7,900

Stockholders' Equity

Common stock	$	10,000		
Retained earnings	$	1,008		
TOTAL STOCKHOLDERS' EQUITY			$	11,008
TOTAL LIABILITIES PLUS TOTAL EQUITY			$	18,908

fig. 49

The value of retained earnings is tracked from period to period using the retained earnings statement. If Corporation X's second quarter resulted in a net profit of $1,000,000 and another $500,000 dividend payout, then the second quarter retained earnings statement might look something like this (figure 50):

Corporation X
Retained Earnings Statement
End of Second Quarter (all dollar amounts in thousands)

Retained Earnings at the beginning of the period	$	1,008
Plus: Net income	$	1,000
	$	2,008
Less: Dividends issued	$	500
Retained Earnings at the end of the period	$	1,508

fig. 50

Chapter Recap

» Assets = Liabilities + Equity is the fundamental accounting equation and provides an essential framework for the practice of double-entry accounting.

» Patents, trademarks, copyrights, and goodwill are examples of intangible assets.

» Certain intangible assets, such as licensing and patents, may be gradually written off as expenses through amortization, a process similar to the writing off of depreciation expenses following the purchase of tangible equipment.

» Every double-entry accounting transaction involves at least one debit and at least one credit.

» In accrual-based accounting, revenues are recorded when revenue is earned, and expenses are recorded when expenses are incurred— these transactions are recorded regardless of when payment is made and received.

» A business's equity accounts include revenue, expense, and accounts that track the flow of capital from and to owners and shareholders.

| 5 |
Recording Business Transactions

Accountants are cowboys of information.

— DAVID FOSTER WALLACE, novelist

Now that you understand the fundamental accounting equation and double-entry accounting, you can rest easy, having put many of accounting's mathematical challenges behind you. As strange as it may seem, accounting does not involve a lot of difficult math. It is mostly just addition and subtraction. The real challenges of accounting, rather than mathematical, are organizational and analytical. An accountant makes him- or herself invaluable by organizing financial data in such a way that it shines a light forward, identifying the business's current direction, needs, and options.

In this chapter we will review several of the specific methods and tools used by accountants and bookkeepers to identify relevant data and to keep this data organized and accurate. Business owners, after reading this chapter, will know what their accountant means when she says she needs to make a "journal entry" or create a "trial balance." If you are a business owner wishing to do your own accounting, this chapter provides key insight for gaining control of your books.

Source Documents

Source documents are the primary records used to verify that a change must be made to one or more accounts. If I own a crop dusting business and my airplane needs its propeller replaced, then my order slip from the propeller manufacturer is my source document, verifying that I have purchased a replacement part for one of my assets. Similarly, if I write a check to the chemical company for 100 pounds of pesticide, then that check could suffice as a source document for my purchase of materials.

Examples of source documents may include the following:

- » Order sheets/sales slips/invoices
- » Receipts
- » Bank statements
- » Checks
- » Bills
- » Credit card statements
- » Time cards/sheets
- » Packing slips
- » Deposit slips

Source documents usually include a description of the products or services, an amount of money owed or paid, and some type of authorization like a signature, stamp, or logo that identifies the other party in the transaction.

Journal Entries and Formal Ledgers

Before accounting transactions are added to ledgers, such as those featured in chapter 4, they are first "journalized." A *journal entry* notates the debit (on the left side) and the credit (on the right) of accounts that are affected by a transaction. Notice how the standard format for an accounting journal keeps credits on the right and also one space below the correlating debit entry. This added differentiation is intended to further separate debits and credits from one another and reduce the chance of a mix-up:

fig. 51

ENTRY YEAR	ENTRY DATE	ACCOUNT	DEBIT	CREDIT
2018	March 31	Dividends	500,000	
		Cash		500,000
	April 1	Expense	102,500	
		Accrued Payroll		102,500
		Expense	63,000	
		Insurance Premium		63,000
	April 4	Cash	385,000	
		Sales Revenue		385,000

Journalizing is important in accounting because it provides a way to trace transactions across chronological timelines. As you may have guessed, businesses, even small ones, usually have many, many accounts, more than we could hope to track accurately using our sample ledgers from the previous chapter. These accounts are tracked on an ongoing basis through the use of computer software or through a robust filing system. Each account, regardless of whether it is an asset, liability, or equity account, has a current balance and a transaction history, all of it derived from the journal entries made, which were themselves derived from source documents. This collection of account data is known collectively as the "ledger" or the "*general ledger.*"

Here is a sample of what a general ledger might look like:

GRAPHIC

fig. 52

GENERAL LEDGER FOR BECKY'S DONUT SHOP

CASH

AUG 1st 100,000	AUG 3rd	4,500
7th	4,235	5th	25,000
10th	3,910	10th	500
13th	150	10th	1,320
13th	4,690	13th	750
		13th	3,200
BAL	77,715		

SECURITY DEPOSITS

| AUG 3rd | 3,000 | AUG 10th | 3,000 |
| BAL | 0 | | |

PREPAID EXPENSE

| AUG 10th | 3,500 | AUG 13th | 3,500 |
| BAL | 0 | | |

EQUIPMENT

| AUG 5th | 25,000 | | |
| BAL | 25,000 | | |

ACCOUNTS PAYABLE

AUG 13th	750	AUG 7th	750
		13th	276
		13th	1,030
		BAL	1,306

ACCRUED PAYROLL

AUG 10th	1,320	AUG 7th	630
		10th	690
		13th	720
		BAL	720

OWNER'S CONTRIBUTIONS

| | | AUG 1st | 100,000 |
| | | BAL | 100,000 |

OWNER'S WITHDRAWALS

| AUG 13th | 3,200 | | |
| BAL | 3,200 | | |

EXPENSE

AUG 3rd	1,500	
7th	750	
7th	630	
10th	690	
13th	276	
13th	3,350	
13th	720	
13th	1,030	
BAL	8,946	

REVENUE

	AUG 7th	4,235
	10th	3,910
	13th	4,690
	BAL	12,835

Notice how debits stay on the left and credits on the right in both the journal entries and ledgers, and how all asset accounts are inclined to have debit balances, whereas all liability accounts and equity accounts (excluding owner's withdrawals and expenses) are inclined to have credit balances.

In the real world, journal entries are usually either fully automated or entered into a software program by an accountant or bookkeeper. The general ledger is updated, maintained, and accessed electronically. Physical source documents can be important to maintain for tax purposes, and some businesses also like to file printouts of their journal entries and ledgers.

NOTE

Even though much of accounting can be managed via computer software, it is still important to maintain a basic accounting filing system for physical receipts and other sensitive paperwork. Many small businesses can accommodate their accounting records using only four filing cabinets: one for assets, one for liabilities, another for equity, and the fourth for owner's capital accounts. Divide the equity cabinet in two, using one half for expenses and the other half for revenue. The cost of four filing cabinets to get your business financially organized is a small price to pay.

Chart of Accounts

In the examples we have used to illustrate the principles of accounting, we have for simplicity's sake underrepresented the quantity of accounts typically maintained by an average business. Even a small business like Becky's Donut Shop is likely to have twenty or thirty different accounts in action at any given time. Large companies are likely to have several thousand accounts, with hundreds of accountants on their payroll.

The number of accounts a business chooses to maintain reflects the level of differentiation desired by the company's management. The accounts payable account from figure 52 could easily be differentiated into two, three, or more separate accounts depending on how many suppliers do business with Becky's Donut Shop. Becky may decide to set up an account for each supplier, or an account for each product type. If Becky decides to partner with her cousin, Noreen, who wants to buy into her donut shop business, then separate accounts will likely be set up to track Noreen's capital contributions and withdrawals from the business.

The ***chart of accounts*** is an expandable list of all accounts maintained by the business. The rudimentary filing structure for the chart of accounts may look something like this:

101-199	Asset accounts
201-299	Liability accounts
301-399	Equity accounts
401-499	Revenue accounts
501-599	Expense accounts

Using this structure, were we to assign account numbers to the accounts we have currently set up for Becky's Donut Shop, we would have the following filing structure:

101	Cash	301	Owner's contributions
102	Security deposits	302	Owner's withdrawals
103	Prepaid expenses		
104	Equipment	401	Revenue
201	Accounts payable	501	Expense
202	Accrued payroll		

If Becky decides that she wants a separate asset account for display cases and furniture, it is easy to set up an account 105 called "furniture." If she wants to track expenses that go to payroll, then she can create an account 502, "payroll expense." If her cousin Noreen buys into the business, then accounts 301 and 302 can be renamed "Owner's contributions – Becky Robinson" and "Owner's withdrawals – Becky Robinson." And new accounts 303 and 304 can be added to track Noreen's equity-related activities.

In our structure, there are 100 available account types under each big-bucket category. For small businesses, this level of account differentiation should be more than adequate. Our three-digit account numbers can be quite informative in a few ways. Obviously, the first digit tells us immediately what kind of account we are dealing with. If we are working with an account that begins with the number 4, we know instantly that it is a revenue account, and that its value will increase on the right side via credits. We can also use the second digit to provide information. For example, we could assign a special significance to all accounts that begin with the digit sequence 1, 0.

101	Cash – Smith's Bank checking
102	Cash – Smith's Bank savings
103	Cash – in safe – Bloomfield location
104	Cash – in safe – Martindale location
105	Cash – in safe – Leesburg location
106	Cash-equivalent investments
…	

Every account beginning with a 10 represents not only an asset, but a cash asset or a cash-equivalent asset. If we are running a larger business and want to differentiate and subcategorize to an even greater degree, then we may want to use four digits rather than three to label our accounts.

NOTE

As a best practice, think about and build out your chart of accounts before you begin entering data and filing.

It is important to choose names for your accounts that are clear and specific. Once the name is established it should be used faithfully throughout every step of your accounting processes. An incorrect or ambiguous account name on a journal entry can easily cause an error in both your journal and your ledger.

In addition to the general ledger (figure 53) which features all asset, liability, and equity accounts, businesses may create and use other ledgers that focus on particular areas of the business. Sales ledgers, for example, may be used to visualize various revenue streams. Purchase ledgers can be used to visualize the company's spending. The general ledger is unique, however, in that it lists all accounts maintained by the business. When all of the debit balances shown on the general ledger are totaled, they should equal the total of all the credit balances.

Trial Balance

Let's revisit our general ledger from Becky's Donut Shop.

fig. 53

GENERAL LEDGER FOR BECKY'S DONUT SHOP		

CASH

AUG 1st	100,000	AUG 3rd	4,500
7th	4,235	5th	25,000
10th	3,910	10th	500
13th	150	10th	1,320
13th	4,690	13th	750
		13th	3,200
BAL	77,715		

SECURITY DEPOSITS

AUG 3rd	3,000	AUG 10th	3,000
BAL	0		

PREPAID EXPENSE

AUG 10th	3,500	AUG 13th	3,500
BAL	0		

EQUIPMENT

AUG 5th	25,000		
BAL	25,000		

ACCOUNTS PAYABLE

AUG 13th	750	AUG 7th	750
		13th	276
		13th	1,030
		BAL	1,306

ACCRUED PAYROLL

AUG 10th	1,320	AUG 7th	630
		10th	690
		13th	720
		BAL	720

OWNER'S CONTRIBUTIONS

	AUG 1st	100,000
	BAL	100,000

OWNER'S WITHDRAWALS

AUG 13th	3,200	
BAL	3,200	

EXPENSE

AUG 3rd	1,500	
7th	750	
7th	630	
10th	690	
13th	276	
13th	3,350	
13th	720	
13th	1,030	
BAL	8,946	

REVENUE

	AUG 7th	4,235
	10th	3,910
	13th	4,690
	BAL	12,835

The total of every debit (left-side) balance can be calculated by adding 77,715 + 25,000 + 3,200 + 8,946 for a total of 114,861. When we total every credit (right-side) balance, 1,306 + 720 + 100,000 + 12,835, we also come to a total of 114,861.

The process of verifying the accuracy of accounts by ensuring that total debit balances are equal to total credit balances is known as creating a ***trial balance*** (figure 54).

Notice that the total of all debit balances ($277,000) is equal to the total of all credit balances (also $277,000). The number $277,000 has no real relevance in and of itself; it's just a measurement of the balance held between the accounts in the business.

When the trial balances equal out, it is a good thing, but it is not an ironclad guarantee that no accounting errors have been made. If an equal quantity of credit and debit entries are made to the wrong account, the trial balance will still show up as equal. Trial balances will also still show up as equal if a single erroneous number is used to determine both a debit and a credit entry. And since double-entry accounting involves making entries in pairs, this type of error is always possible. Nevertheless, the trial balance remains a useful method for detecting and correcting accounting errors.

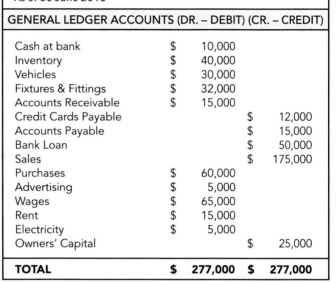

Trial Balance

XYZ Trading

As of 30 June 2010

GENERAL LEDGER ACCOUNTS (DR. – DEBIT) (CR. – CREDIT)		
Cash at bank	$ 10,000	
Inventory	$ 40,000	
Vehicles	$ 30,000	
Fixtures & Fittings	$ 32,000	
Accounts Receivable	$ 15,000	
Credit Cards Payable		$ 12,000
Accounts Payable		$ 15,000
Bank Loan		$ 50,000
Sales		$ 175,000
Purchases	$ 60,000	
Advertising	$ 5,000	
Wages	$ 65,000	
Rent	$ 15,000	
Electricity	$ 5,000	
Owners' Capital		$ 25,000
TOTAL	**$ 277,000**	**$ 277,000**

GRAPHIC

fig. 54

REMEMBER

When your debit balances are not equal to your credit balances, note the amount of the discrepancy. Use this information to search out transactions that may have been omitted or entered incorrectly in the journal or ledger.

When your total debits are not equal to your total credits, then you have an accounting problem that must be investigated. There is a specific process for investigating erroneous trial balances with maximum efficiency:

» **Step 1**: Check the arithmetic. Hopefully, the reason the totals aren't equal is because someone simply punched an incorrect number into his or her calculator when adding one of the columns.

» **Step 2**: If your arithmetic checks out but there is still an error, then go back to the account ledgers that were used and double-check the balance amount listed for each account. If you did not record the correct balance, that is likely the cause of your error.

» **Step 3**: Check to see if a debit entry was listed as a credit (or a credit entry listed as a debit). Such a mistake would obviously throw off your numbers. In fact, if this is your only error, then the difference between your disparate balances equals twice the value of the erroneously entered account balance. For example, in the figure 54 trial balance, had you listed the advertising expense account of $5,000 as a credit balance rather than a debit balance, then your debit/credit totals would have been $272,000/$282,000, a difference of $10,000, or $5,000 times 2.

» **Step 4**: If you are still unable to reconcile your balances, then you need to bite the bullet and go through each ledger and recompute its account balance.

» **Step 5**: Check to make sure that all journal entries were posted properly to their ledgers.

» **Step 6**: Verify that each original journal entry consists of equal amounts credited and debited.

Prepaid Expenses & Unearned Revenues

In accrual-based accounting, certain revenues and expenses are recorded incrementally rather than all at once. A personal injury attorney, for example, may pay an advertising agency $15,000 for a promotional package that guarantees his ads will run steadily over the next six months during daytime TV programming. If the attorney pays the $15,000 before the six-month advertising period begins, then the entry will be treated as a "prepaid expense." The journal entry will debit the prepaid advertising (asset account) and credit the cash (asset account).

fig. 55

ENTRY DATE	ACCOUNT	DEBIT	CREDIT
2018 Jan 31	Prepaid Advertising	15,000	
	Cash		15,000

If we assume that the advertisements will run from February 1 through July 31, then in theory, the cost for each month of advertising will be $2,500. When the attorney's accountant prepares his end-of-month financial statements for February, he will make an "adjusting entry" to reflect the $2,500 worth of advertising that was consumed over the last month (figure 56).

If the attorney's accountant prepares financial statements on a monthly basis, then he will continue to make what are known as ***adjusting entries***— debiting advertising expense by $2,500 and crediting prepaid advertising by $2,500—until the prepaid advertising account has a balance of zero.

fig. 56

ENTRY DATE	ACCOUNT	DEBIT	CREDIT
2018 Jan 31	Prepaid Advertising	15,000	
	Cash		15,000
2018 Feb 28	Advertising Expense	2,500	
	Prepaid Advertising		2,500

Other examples of prepaid expenses that, under accrual accounting, must be gradually credited out of assets include, but are not limited to, prepaid insurance, prepaid rent, and prepaid supplies.

Similar to—but opposite from—accounting for prepaid expenses is accounting for unearned revenues. The advertising company that sells the six month's worth of daytime TV commercials to the personal injury attorney is receiving $15,000 before they deliver a product. The ad company's accountant will treat this income as "unearned revenue." The cash (asset account) is debited and the unearned revenue (liability account) is credited.

fig. 57

ENTRY DATE	ACCOUNT	DEBIT	CREDIT
2018 Jan 31	Cash	15,000	
	Unearned Revenue		15,000

After the first month's worth of advertising service is provided, the advertising company will debit the unearned revenue (liability account) by $2,500 and credit their earnings account by the same amount.

fig. 58

ENTRY DATE	ACCOUNT	DEBIT	CREDIT
2018 Jan 31	Cash	15,000	
	Unearned Revenue		15,000
	Unearned Revenue	2,500	
	Sales Revenue		2,500

One of the principal advantages of accrual accounting over cash accounting is that it allows businesses to visualize their actual expenses and actual revenues in a way that reflects the flow of business rather than only the flow of cash.

In our example, adjusting entries are made every month to reflect the delivery and consumption of advertising services that have already been paid for. Why one month? Why not make adjusting entries every week or every day? The period of time between adjusting entries is determined simply by the business's defined accounting periods. In our example, it can be assumed that the business tracks its financials and generates major financial statements on a monthly basis. Hence, all adjusting entries must be made when the statements are issued at the end of the month. If you are wondering how to determine an appropriate interval of time between adjusting entries, simply refer to the normal time frames your business uses to define accounting periods.

NOTE

There is a basic assumption in accounting known as the "periodicity assumption," which asserts that the life of a business can be adequately represented using arbitrary snippets of time—months, quarters, years, fiscal years, etc.—and that useful financial statements can be created to reflect these periods.

Accounting periods are defined and modified at the discretion of business management. Accounting periods can be determined unilaterally by the business's CEO, or the task may be deferred to the wisdom of the company's *chief financial officer (CFO)*, usually an accountant. If the business contracts out its accounting services to a third party, then that accounting firm or individual accountant may determine or advise on appropriate accounting periods.

Making adjusting entries is not always as simple as taking a prepaid expense or unearned revenue and dividing it up evenly across several accounting periods. Adjusting entries should accurately reflect the usage of the asset (or the servicing of the liability) that occurred during the accounting period. If a painting business purchases what it estimates to be a year's worth of painting supplies for $17,000 but ends up using 30 percent of the supplies within the first month following the purchase, then the adjusting entry at the end of the first month (assuming the business uses monthly accounting periods) should debit $5,100 (.30 x $17,000) in supplies expense and credit $5,100 out of the prepaid supply asset account.

GRAPHIC

fig. 59

ENTRY DATE	ACCOUNT	DEBIT	CREDIT
2019 Jul 31	Prepaid Supplies	17,000	
	Cash		17,000
2019 Aug 31	Supplies Expense	5,100	
	Prepaid Supplies		5,100

If there are only a small number of jobs in September and the painting company only uses $1,000 worth of supplies, then that amount must be journaled.

ENTRY DATE	ACCOUNT	DEBIT	CREDIT
2019 Jul 31	Prepaid Supplies	17,000	
	Cash		17,000
2019 Aug 31	Supplies Expense	5,100	
	Prepaid Supplies		5,100
2019 Sept 31	Supplies Expense	1,000	
	Prepaid Supplies		1,000

REMEMBER

The journal entries feed the ledger, and the ledger is used to generate financial statements.

Adjusting journal entries are made at the end of established accounting periods, because alternative approaches would prove unfeasible. It would be incredibly time-consuming for accountants to worry about making adjusting entries every time any quantity of prepaid assets was consumed. Imagine the bookkeeper for the painting business having to define a dollar value for the quantity of painting supplies consumed on a day-by-day basis. It would be tedious at best, ridiculous at worst.

Or would it be? Perhaps not the painting business, but indeed, *some* businesses keep incredibly precise day-by-day and even hour-by-hour records of supplies and materials. These complex, high-tech accounting systems are more commonly found in managerial accounting than in financial accounting. In chapter 6 we will take a closer look at managerial accounting and how it adds a unique dimension to the accounting landscape.

DIGITAL ASSETS

HANDS-ON LEARNING: Further analysis and additional examples of adjusting entries can be found in my online accounting course, including a discussion and illustration of *reversing entries*.

Chapter Recap

» Source documents inform necessary changes to accounting records.

» Through the use of journal entries, accountants and bookkeepers construct chronological records of relevant transactions.

» Ledgers contain ongoing compilations of account data, plus current balances for all accounts maintained by a business.

» Using a chart of accounts and numerical encoding, accounts can be organized and delineated into various expandable categories.

» A trial balance is a listing of all account balances at a given time; debit balances should be equal to credit balances.

» Adjusting entries record the incremental consumption of prepaid assets and the incremental earning of unearned revenue.

» Adjusting entries should be added to accounting records at the end of each accounting period, immediately preceding the creation of financial statements.

| 6 |

Managerial Accounting
How to Put Accounting Fundamentals to Work on Behalf of Your Business

Chapter Overview
>> CVP Analysis
>> Product and Period Costs
>> Break-Even Points
>> Target Income
>> Multi-Product Analysis
>> Inventory
>> Budgeting

Balanced budget requirements seem more likely to produce accounting ingenuity than genuinely balanced budgets.
— THOMAS SOWELL, American economist

Managerial accounting expands the principles of accounting beyond the financial realm into the logistical and strategic dimensions of business decision-making. An industrial parts supplier decides to expand its warehousing capacity. Would it be more efficient to invest in a new warehouse? Or should the company expand its current warehouse by adding on a new floor? How much storage capacity is gained in either scenario, and at what cost? Which option offers the best return on investment?

The purpose of managerial accounting is to help business managers make better decisions. A key differentiator that separates managerial accounting from financial accounting is the intended audience. In managerial accounting, the intended audience is the decision-makers within the business. In financial accounting, the intended audience is usually an external one—investors, auditors, bondholders, etc. The methods used in financial accounting are often highly standardized and are subject to GAAP (chapter 7) and various other compliance requirements. Managerial accounting methods, by contrast, are highly customized and are tailored with a great deal of precision to the immediate needs of the business.

Managerial accounting constantly evolves within an organization. The development and maintenance of optimized managerial accounting practices require cycles of evaluation, updates, and reimplementation. An ice cream store has a display freezer with a capacity to offer only twenty different ice cream flavors. The business owner tracks the sales of every ice cream flavor. Every three months, the five flavors with the poorest sales record are swapped out for five new flavors. Meanwhile, the ice cream shop owner may discover that he sells four times as much strawberry swirl as butter pecan. After evaluating this data, he will likely decide to purchase more strawberry swirl so he can meet the high demand. In time, the ice cream wholesaler may discover the high demand for his product, and he might raise its price. The ice cream shop owner would then need to evaluate again, deciding either to accept a lower profit margin or to raise the retail price of strawberry swirl and thus accept the risk of diminished sales.

While our ice cream shop owner is not likely to have a hyper-sophisticated managerial accounting system in place, there are certain mechanisms he could use to increase his likelihood of finding the perfect price for strawberry swirl as well as his other products. In this chapter we will review a few practical managerial accounting techniques that can help business owners make better decisions.

Cost-Volume-Profit (CVP) Analysis

Accounting for the costs associated with providing goods and services and analyzing how these costs affect profits is central to managerial accounting. Most small business owners, though they understand that costs affect their bottom line, neglect to conduct even rudimentary analyses of their cost strategy. Good managerial accounting practice allows businesses better vantage points for their negotiations, greater insight into which products and services are most (and least) profitable, and the ability to determine with precision the point at which the business's sales revenues are sufficient to cover both its variable and fixed costs within a given accounting period—the "break-even" point. The study of the interplay between the costs of goods and services, sales quantities, and profit is known as *cost–volume–profit (CVP) analysis*.

CVP analysis is informed by a multitude of components, some of which you are likely already familiar with, such as "variable" and "fixed" costs. Variable costs increase in direct proportion to the volume of products sold or services rendered. If a professional masseuse uses an exotic lavender oil each time she gives a massage, then the cost of the lavender oil (over a given period of time) will increase in direct proportion to the quantity (volume) of massages given. The cost of the oil is a variable cost. The masseuse's phone, internet, and rent expenses are fixed costs, as they remain the same regardless of client volume.

When a product or service is sold, the **contribution margin** refers to the quantity of revenue left over after all variable costs are accounted for. If a hamburger is sold for $3 and the cost of the ingredients used to make the hamburger is $1, then the contribution margin for the hamburger is $2. If one hundred of these hamburgers are sold, then $300 of revenue is collected, $100 worth of costs are incurred, and the total contribution margin is $200.

The contribution margin is so named because this amount *contributes* to the business's *fixed* costs. The $200 left over after selling a hundred hamburgers can be applied to the restaurant's rent, utility bills, manager's salary, and other fixed costs. Let's assume that for a given period the hamburger restaurant's fixed costs total $1,000. The restaurant must sell 500 hamburgers during this period in order to pay for its fixed costs. Once 500 hamburgers are sold, the restaurant's fixed (and variable) costs are covered. The break-even point has been reached. The contribution margin from any additional sales during this period represents pure profit.

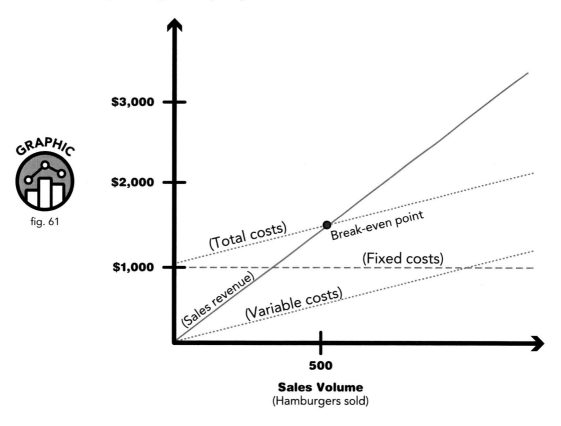

GRAPHIC

fig. 61

$3,000

$2,000

(Total costs)   Break-even point

(Fixed costs)

$1,000

(Sales revenue)   (Variable costs)

500

Sales Volume
(Hamburgers sold)

Figure 61 illustrates the relationship between sales volume, cost, and profit. To understand the graphic, first take note of the relationship between sales revenue and variable costs. Each hamburger sold generates $3 in sales revenue and $1 in variable costs. By the time we reach $1,000 in sales revenue (after about 333 burgers are sold) we probably have enough cash on hand to pay rent, utilities, and other fixed costs for the period. Nevertheless, we have not yet turned a profit, because we haven't generated enough revenue to cover our variable costs. If you study the "total costs" line on the figure 61 graph, you will notice that its value is always equal to $1,000 (total fixed costs) + the value of variable costs. At 500 hamburgers, variable costs are $500 ($1 per burger), and total costs are $1,500 ($1,000 + $500). This is the point at which total sales revenue is equal to total costs, the break-even point. Each hamburger sold after 500 contributes $2 to the business's overall profitability for the period. In fact, we can expand our figure 61 graph to model profit and loss.

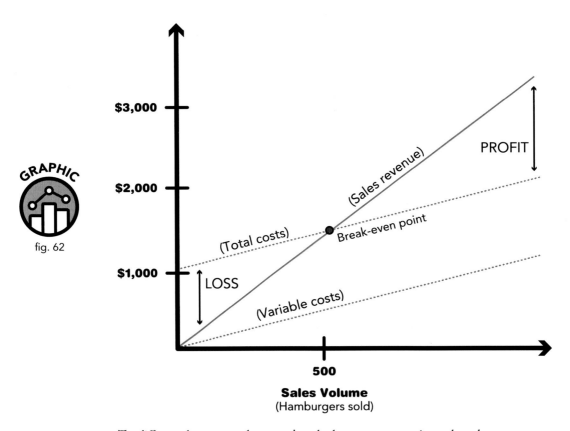

fig. 62

The difference between total costs and total sales revenue t any given sales volume represents the business's profit or loss.

In chapters 2 and 3 we explored the accounting practices of Kathi's Jewelry Design business. As you may recall, Kathi is a sole proprietor who sells handcrafted jewelry through online retail channels and, more recently, through a newly opened brick-and-mortar storefront. She pays rent, has a few employees, and relies on wholesalers to provide the component materials needed to create the products in her signature jewelry line. Component materials include gemstones, bands, chains, boxes, etc. These materials are considered "product costs" because they are integral to the products being sold. *Product costs* are defined simply as the costs expended in the creation of a product or the delivery of a service; they can include more than just raw materials. The commission payment made to a salesman is a product cost if the expense of the labor can be attributed directly to the creation or sale of a specific product. Product costs may also be broader in scope. If a sprocket company devotes an entire factory to the creation of a certain type of sprocket, then the factory overhead expense may be considered a product cost for managerial accounting purposes.

Period costs are more closely associated with the passage of time and cannot be attributed to the production or delivery of a specific product or service. The rent Kathi pays for her storefront is a period cost, as well as her advertising expense, general supplies expense, and insurance expense. Wage and salary expense can be either product costs or period costs depending on the extent to which the labor can be tracked to a particular product or service. Kathi herself is the business's principal artisan and personally crafts the bulk of her own product line. She relies on her staff for sales service, general store upkeep, and assistance with jewelry cleaning and repair orders. As a small business owner with very modest levels of accounting sophistication, Kathi finds it easier to treat payroll as a period cost rather than a product cost. Now, let's say that Kathi wanted to introduce a new line of colorfully hand-painted wooden rings, and she found a local artist willing to contract out his painting services. Perhaps they agree to a fee of $75 per ring painted. This contract labor cost would clearly be a product cost rather than a period cost.

The distinction between product costs and period costs is important to managerial accounting, because it determines when expenses are recorded and when they show up on the business's income statement. Product costs are generally handled similarly to inventory costs. In fact, in some accounting nomenclature, product costs may also be referred to as "inventoriable costs" or "direct labor costs." Unlike financial accounting, managerial accounting is highly customizable, and businesses may choose from a variety of different cost classification systems. Fundamentally, however, product costs are not recorded as expenses until the product itself is sold. Let's say that Kathi sells her rings for $150 apiece. We already know that each ring has $75 in contract labor attached to it. For a small business like Kathi's, the simplest managerial accounting approach is to treat the $75 as a part of inventory cost. If the wooden rings (before being painted) cost $5 per unit to acquire, then the total value of each ring (as an asset) is $80. The rings are accounted for as assets until they are sold, at which point the inventory (asset account) is credited by $80 per ring sold, and the expense (equity account) is debited by $80 per ring sold. Assuming Kathi sticks to her $150 price point for each ring, the cash (asset account) is debited by $150 per ring, and the revenue (equity account) is credited by the same amount. By incorporating product costs (aka inventoriable costs or direct labor costs) into inventory, businesses can benefit from more precise financial data.

As you may have noted, *product* and *period* costs are somewhat analogous to *variable* and *fixed* costs, respectively. As with many aspects of managerial accounting, businesses may select from a wide variety of methods and nomenclatures. The terms *product* costs and *period* costs are more prevalent in the industrial manufacturing industry, where managers are constantly accounting for costs associated with production line management, energy consumption, and the unit-by-unit price of raw materials. The terms *variable* costs and *fixed* costs, by contrast, are more universal.

Keeping It Simple

Managerial accounting has an unfortunate knack for turning off a lot of accounting students, due to its apparent complexity. Whereas financial accounting is highly standardized and fairly intuitive once you get the hang of it, managerial accounting can feel a lot less tame and less accessible. As mentioned previously, there are more opportunities for creativity and customization in managerial accounting; there are many different rabbit holes to follow. Our purpose in this book is to provide a basic overview of managerial accounting, which is fairly difficult to do given the enormous breadth of the subject, but let's give it a shot.

Much of managerial accounting's practical value stems from its ability to inform business decisions. Which products should a business sell? Which services should it offer? And at what price?

The cost-volume-profit analysis discussed in the previous section can be modeled using a fairly simple equation:

Sales Revenue − Variable Costs − Fixed Costs = Profit

We can unpack "sales revenue" and express it as units sold multiplied by sales price, and we can also unpack variable costs and express it as units sold multiplied by cost per unit.

A surfboard shop sells surfboards for $150 each at a cost of $50 per unit. Over a one-month period the shop sells 75 surfboards and has fixed costs of $3,000.

$$\textbf{Profit} = (\$150*75) - (\$50*75) - \$3,000 = \textbf{\$4,500}$$

This simple formula can be used in many ways. Let's say that the surf shop owner from our example wants to know how many surfboards he needs to sell to reach his break-even point. When a business is at its break-even point, its profit is at exactly zero, as all variable and fixed expenses have been paid for, and the business has turned neither a profit nor a loss. To calculate the number of products that need to be sold in order to reach the break-even point, we simply set the profit value in our equation to zero and use simple algebra to solve for the units (u).

$$\$150u - \$50u - \$3,000 = \$0$$
$$\$100u - \$3,000 = \$0$$
$$\$100u = \$3,000$$
$$u = 30$$

Thanks to our analysis, we now know how many units need to be sold in order for the business to break even. Extrapolating from our calculations, we can deduce that the business must earn $4,500 in revenue ($150*30) from surfboard sales in order to cover its variable and fixed expenses.

When conducting break-even analyses and using the managerial accounting equation in general, it is helpful to always keep in mind the concept of the contribution margin. In our example, every surfboard sold offers a contribution of $100 toward the business's fixed expenses. Once these expenses are accounted for, the business has broken even and is free to start turning a profit. We know we have $3,000 in fixed expenses to account for and that each surfboard sale contributes $100; simply divide $3,000 by $100 to quickly arrive at the break-even unit sales target of 30.

This basic managerial accounting formula may also be used to set **target income** goals. Target income is the amount of money (profit) a business seeks to make in order to attain its financial objectives. For the manager of a small business, like a jewelry maker or surfboard shop owner, the target income is essentially the amount of money that the owner wants to make from his or her business. For larger businesses, target income may be based on the business's desire to pay out dividends to its shareholders, pay down debt, or satisfy the expectations of analysts. Ultimately, target income is whatever the business decision-makers want it to be. Let's say, for instance, that our surf shop owner wants to stop paying rent and is looking to purchase his current business location from his landlord. He will need to make a $100,000 down payment in order to accomplish his goal, and he wants to amass enough money to make this payment within the next twelve months. He'll need to make about $8,333.33 per month in addition to providing for his own personal living needs and those of his family. He decides to set a target income for his business at $14,000 per month. How many surfboards does he have to sell?

$$\$14,000 = \$150u - \$50u - \$3,000$$
$$\$14,000 = \$100u - \$3,000$$
$$\$17,000 = \$100u$$
$$170 = u$$

He needs to sell 170 surfboards on a monthly basis for twelve months. It is definitely a tall order, considering that the shop has been selling about 75 a month on average. But our surf shop owner, let's call him Gus, is a determined fellow and is willing to consider several options for solving his financial dilemma.

Obviously, Gus would like to sell more surfboards, but he doesn't think it's reasonable to expect to double his sales overnight. Maybe with a few well-placed ads and more competitive sales commissions for his staff members, he can invest his way into a 25 percent jump in sales. But the extra advertising costs will add an additional $500 to Gus's fixed costs, and the sales commissions (product costs) will make it more expensive to sell each surfboard. The variable cost per board sold will climb from $50 to $65. Gus knows he will need to raise the price on his surfboards, but he is wary of driving customers to his competitors. He decides that a 15 percent price hike is the most that his customers will tolerate. The new price per surfboard is $172.50, and Gus expects to sell about 95 units, thanks to his new sales efforts.

Gus's Average Profit = ($150*75) − ($50*75) − $3,000 = $4,500
Gus's New Projected Profit = ($172.50*95) − ($65*95) − $3,500 = $6,712.50

Notice that the total contribution margin for all sales, previously ($150*75) – ($50*75) or $7,500, is now projected to be ($172.50*95) – ($65*95) or $10,212.50. The per-unit contribution margin went from $150 – $50 ($100) to $172.50 – $65 ($107.50). Notice how a fairly modest difference in the total contribution margin, when accompanied by a modest 25 percent increase in sales numbers, has the power to boost profits by nearly 50 percent. Gus is still short of his target income of $14,000, but he is moving in the right direction.

When managerial accountants strategize new ways to build profit, they often tinker with more than one variable at a time. A basic strategy for success is to maximize sales on products and services that yield the greatest contribution margins.

Multi-Product Analysis

Understanding the basics of CVP-based managerial accounting is easiest when you assume there is only one product (or product category) being sold. In the real world, as we all know, businesses sell a multitude of different products, at different contribution margins. The good news is that it is actually not that hard to incorporate multiple products into your CVP models.

Take Kathi's jewelry business. Let's say her product line includes jewel-adorned gold bracelets, pearl necklaces, and the hand-painted wooden rings (which, as we know, cost $80 per unit and sell for $150).

fig. 63

PRODUCT	COST PER UNIT	SALES PRICE	CONTRIBUTION MARGIN PER UNIT
Wooden Rings	$ 80	$ 150	$ 70
Bracelets	$ 20	$ 100	$ 80
Necklaces	$ 10	$ 65	$ 55

Whether we are working with three or three hundred different products, if we want to employ the power of CVP analysis on our behalf, then we need to first carry out a basic analysis called a "sales mix." A sales mix analysis essentially involves determining how much sales revenue (and how much profit) is flowing into the business from the sale of various products.

fig. 64

	SALES MIX			**TOTAL SALES**
	Wooden Rings	Bracelets	Necklaces	Total Units Sold
Units sold	36	23	19	**78**
Sales revenue	$ 5,400	$ 2,300	$ 1,235	$ 8,935
Cost	$ 2,880	$ 460	$ 190	$ 3,530
Contribution margin	$ 2,520	$ 1,840	$ 1,045	$ 5,405

The preceding table tells us that the biggest drivers of sales revenue and contribution margin are Kathi's wooden rings. Nice to know, but how do we apply this information to the betterment of the business? In order to maximize the usefulness of a sales mix analysis, it helps to express contribution margin as a percentage. Wooden rings, for instance, contribute $70 from their $150 sales price to the business's fixed expenses, a contribution margin of 47 percent (70/150). Let's calculate the contribution margin percentages for all three of Kathi's products. While we are at it, we should also chart each product's sales revenue percentage as it relates to total sales revenue.

GRAPHIC

fig. 65

	SALES MIX			**TOTAL SALES**
	Wooden Rings	Bracelets	Necklaces	Total Units Sold
Units sold	36	23	19	78
Sales revenue	$ 5,400	$ 2,300	$ 1,235	$ 8,935
Sales revenue %	60%	26%	14%	
Cost	$ 2,880	$ 460	$ 190	$ 3,530
Contribution margin	$ 2,520	$ 1,840	$ 1,045	$ 5,405
Contribution margin %	47%	80%	85%	60%

Now we have some data we can work with. If you study the table from a managerial accountant's perspective—pretend you are Kathi's CFO—you will notice that Kathi has a clear problem in her sales mix. Sixty percent of her sales revenue is coming from her wooden rings, which have the lowest contribution margin at 47 percent. Think of it this way: for every dollar that comes into the business via the purchase of a wooden ring, only 47 cents can be contributed to the business's fixed costs. Low contribution margins make it harder to break even and, of course, harder to turn a profit and to achieve target incomes.

Take a look at the Total Sales column on the far right of the table. Here we have calculated Kathi's total sales revenue, total cost, and total contribution margin. These data can be plugged in to the standard CVP equation (Sales revenue – Variable costs – Fixed costs = Profit), leaving us again with a simple yet powerful formula that incorporates multiple products and provides us with a look at overall contribution margin as well as overall profitability.

Kathi's overall contribution margin is 60 percent. On average, every dollar of revenue that comes into the business contributes 60 cents to the business's fixed costs. Kathi may find herself a bit frustrated by a 60 percent contribution margin, given that two of her three signature products, bracelets and necklaces, have contribution margins of 80 percent or more.

The obvious solution is to sell more bracelets and necklaces. If Kathi can find a way to bring in about $1,000 more in revenue from her bracelets and another $1,000 more from her necklaces, she can raise her overall contribution margin from $5,405 to $7,030.

fig. 66

	SALES MIX				TOTAL SALES
	Wooden Rings	Bracelets	Necklaces		Total Units Sold
Units sold	36	33	34		**103**
Sales revenue	$ 5,400	$ 3,300	$ 2,210	$	10,910
Sales revenue %	49%	30%	20%		
Cost	$ 2,880	$ 660	$ 340	$	3,880
Contribution margin	$ 2,520	$ 2,640	$ 1,870	$	7,030
Contribution margin %	47%	80%	85%		64%

Notice that the overall contribution margin percent only increases by a modest amount, from 60 percent to 64 percent, due to the fact that sales revenue percentages are still dominated by the wooden rings. Kathi must be careful here. She would love for her bracelets and necklaces to dominate the sales revenue percentages, but *not* if her total sales revenue declines in the process. Remember, every wooden ring sold contributes $70, which is second only to the bracelets in gross contribution margin, per unit sold.

fig. 67

PRODUCT	COST PER UNIT	SALES PRICE	CONTRIBUTION MARGIN PER UNIT
Wooden Rings	$ 80	$ 150	$ 70
Bracelets	$ 20	$ 100	$ 80
Necklaces	$ 10	$ 65	$ 55

When analyzing a sales mix for the purpose of strategic business decision-making, it can be helpful to think in terms of sales revenue, not unit quantity. A competent accountant is not going to advise Kathi to simply focus on selling fewer wooden rings and more bracelets and necklaces in order to raise the overall contribution margin. A better idea would be to run a promotion giving customers who purchase wooden rings a 20 percent or 25 percent (attractive) discount on a bracelet or a necklace. In this way we would bring in more revenue from bracelets and necklaces (both of which can withstand deep discounts and still be profitable) and we would do so without diminishing Kathi's strongest seller, the hand-painted wooden ring.

This is, of course, only one of many strategies that Kathi's accountant may offer. We may also consider raising the price of the wooden ring and thereby raising its contribution margin. We may try to simply push as many bracelets as possible since they have the largest contribution margin per unit. Or, most likely, we will enact several strategies simultaneously, study our results at the end of the next period, set goals, and move forward. This is the business of managerial accounting.

Accounting for Inventory

Simply put, inventory received is debited into the inventory (asset account). When the inventory is sold, it is credited out of the inventory account and the cost of goods sold (expense account) is debited. This method ensures that the expense of the inventory does not show up on the business's income statement until it is sold.

When inventory is received and the inventory account is debited, the accounts payable account is credited (if the recipient does not immediately pay for the inventory delivered) or the cash account is credited (if payment is made immediately).

GRAPHIC

fig. 68

ACCOUNT	DEBIT	CREDIT		ACCOUNT	DEBIT	CREDIT
Inventory	2,700		**OR**	Inventory	2,700	
Accounts Payable		2,700		Cash		2,700

Johnny's Auto Garage receives a shipment of radiators worth $2,700. There are nine radiators in total, each worth $300.

NOTE

For the sake of accurate record-keeping, dispute resolution, and tax preparedness, be sure to request and file a purchase invoice for the inventory you purchase.

Let's say Johnny's Auto Garage is unsatisfied with the merchandise received—one of the radiators is clearly defective. If he is able to return part of the order back to the wholesaler, then the inventory account is credited and the accounts payable or cash account is debited to reflect what is known as a "purchase return."

GRAPHIC

fig. 69

ACCOUNT	DEBIT	CREDIT		ACCOUNT	DEBIT	CREDIT
Accounts Payable	300		**OR**	Cash	300	
Inventory		300		Inventory		300

When a buyer has a problem with goods received, and, rather than return them, negotiates a reduced price, the resulting accounting transaction is known as a "purchase allowance." Again, accounts payable or cash is debited and inventory is credited.

NOTE

In the abnormal event that the defective radiator is completely unusable *and* the wholesaler refuses to issue a full $300 refund (let's say they only issue a $270 refund and expect Johnny to eat the difference, for whatever reason), then $300 is credited out of inventory, $270 is debited into cash, and $30 is debited into an expense account.

When Johnny's Auto Garage retails the radiators (let's say three radiators are retailed at a price of $450 apiece), the cost of goods sold (expense account) is debited for the original $300-per-unit wholesale price and the inventory account is credited. Also, the cash or accounts receivable account is debited and the revenue account is credited to reflect the payment for the goods.

fig. 70

ACCOUNT	DEBIT	CREDIT
Cost of Goods Sold	900	
Inventory		900

AND

ACCOUNT	DEBIT	CREDIT
Cash	1,350	
Revenue		1,350

If your business is charged for the shipment of goods, then the shipping costs must be added (debited) into your inventory asset account and factored into the cost of the products. Shipping costs incurred to obtain inventory are clearly and directly associated with the cost of selling a product. If we assume that Johnny's Auto Garage paid $45 in shipping to receive the nine radiators (at a wholesale price of $300 apiece, $2,700 total before shipping), then we would need to include the additional $45 shipping cost in our accounting as follows:

fig. 71

ACCOUNT	DEBIT	CREDIT
Inventory	2,745	
Accounts Payable		2,745

OR

ACCOUNT	DEBIT	CREDIT
Inventory	2,745	
Cash		2,745

When the garage sells its three radiators, the cost of the shipping must be distributed into the cost of goods sold. Each radiator effectively costs $5 (45/9) to ship. With shipping included, our total cost of goods sold expensed in the transaction is $915 (three radiators at $300 each, plus an additional $15 in associated shipping costs).

fig. 72

ACCOUNT	DEBIT	CREDIT
Cost of Goods Sold	915	
Inventory		915

When a wholesaler or other seller incurs shipping costs while *selling* (as opposed to buying) a product, the seller should record the transaction by debiting the "freight out" or "delivery" (expense account). If the wholesaler of the radiators decides not to charge Johnny's Auto Garage for the delivery cost and decides instead to absorb the $45 expense itself, then the journal entry for the wholesaler might look something like the following:

fig. 73

ACCOUNT	DEBIT	CREDIT
Freight Out Expense	45	
Accounts Payable		45

OR

ACCOUNT	DEBIT	CREDIT
Freight Out Expense	45	
Cash		45

Budgeting

"It's time to prepare a budget."

These words instill fear in even the most fiscally responsible of individuals. Budgeting can seem like a daunting proposition, whether you are managing a home, a sole proprietorship, or a corporation. Yet budgeting is an essential part of managerial accounting, especially for smaller businesses.

Budgeting is about preparing for what is coming next. A disciplined budget allows a manager to exert more control over the direction of their business. The act of budgeting not only helps a manager create a roadmap for moving forward, it also allows them an opportunity to take note of where their business currently stands in terms of the acquisition and expenditure of resources. Once budgets are established, they become a highly useful tool for evaluating the business's performance. In short, budgeting is an important forward-looking planning exercise for a business, as well as a meaningful retrospective evaluation tool.

Not everyone budgets. Some households neglect their budgeting and, certainly, some businesses neglect it as well. Establishing a budget for a business is not as simple as one might think. The spending and earning done by most businesses is affected by the actions of multiple parties. For starters, owners and top-level management must be firmly on board with the budget if it has any chance of being successful. In a case of undisciplined, disinterested, or otherwise uncommitted management, budgeting is a lost cause.

Moving beyond the upper reaches of your business, a budget is much more likely to be respected by team members when they themselves have had a hand in its creation. One way to build participation and consensus in your business is to pursue a "bottom-up" budgeting process. In the bottom-up model, lower-level managers are asked to submit detailed requests for financial resources. These requests are reviewed by upper-level managers who are responsible for signing off on the final budget. This approach is common in larger businesses. Many smaller businesses rely instead on a "top-down" approach to budgeting, where upper-level management creates the budget, acquiring feedback and input from relevant parties as needed. Smaller businesses' tendency toward top-down budgeting can be attributed to the fact that higher-level managers in small businesses are more likely to possess robust knowledge of the intricacies of company operations at all levels.

Why Budget?

Every business should have an overall strategy, one that includes financial goals. A budget establishes specific goals and can even provide a rough financial framework to clarify the path a business must take in order to achieve those goals.

Business owners and managers use budgets to instill a sense of focus and drive, not only in themselves but in their employees as well. A budget put down on paper (or in a table or spreadsheet) offers a roadmap, discernible destination points, and an all-important feedback loop that allows for the tracking and celebration of progress.

Enforcing a budget allows for better overall control of company spending; runaway spending is prevented, or at least checked. While a budget should not quash flexibility or new ideas, it should be used as a management control function. The exertion of managerial control via budgeting need not be overbearing—no one likes a penny counter—but if you can get your employees to buy in to the budget as a measure of achievement, budgeting will boost morale. As previously noted, participation is key. Executives should involve lower-level managers in the creation and implementation of new budgets.

Drafting a budget is also helpful for the purpose of raising capital. Potential investors will undoubtedly be interested in the extent to which a business's proposed budgets reflect a sound strategy for growth and profit.

Types of Budgets in Managerial Accounting

At the core of all budgeting efforts within a business is the ***master budget***. The master budget is the aggregate product of several more narrowly focused budgets, the quantity and nature of which depend on the type of business doing the budgeting. In the various budgets that compose the master budget, all of the three main business activities (discussed in chapter 1) are represented—operating, financing, and investing. In most businesses the master budget is prepared either annually or quarterly.

Operating budgets are often subdivided into component budgets. Operating budgets may encompass sales budgets, production budgets, direct materials budgets, direct labor budgets, manufacturing overhead budgets, marketing budgets, costs of goods sold budgets, selling and administrative expense budgets, and other budgets affecting day-to-day operations of the business.

fig. 74

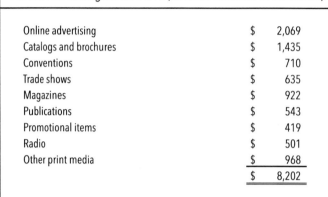

PrintCo
Marketing Budget
For the Year Ending on 12/31/18 (all dollar amounts in thousands)

Online advertising	$	2,069
Catalogs and brochures	$	1,435
Conventions	$	710
Trade shows	$	635
Magazines	$	922
Publications	$	543
Promotional items	$	419
Radio	$	501
Other print media	$	968
	$	8,202

Sample Marketing Budget

Financial budgets in many ways are simply projections of financial statements. You have the "budgeted income statement," which is essentially a standard income statement (see chapter 2) populated with goals and projections as opposed to confirmed financial data. The expectations and goals established by the budgeted income statement speak to more than just the business's anticipated bottom line profit. The statement can be used to project other critical business metrics, such as sales volume and profit margin. Though business owners and managers are free to structure the budgeted income statement differently from the regular income statement, it may be helpful to keep these two statements fairly well aligned in terms of their featured line items. This way, when your accounting software produces "budget vs. actual" reports, it will be an apples-to-apples comparison.

The "budgeted balance sheet" is a record of the business's projected asset, liability, and equity values. It is a view of what the balance sheet will look like if the business performs as planned. The budgeted balance sheet is usually prepared after most or all other components of the master budget have been prepared.

The "cash budget" is the financial budget most similar to the statement of cash flows (chapter 2). In addition to being a projection, a cash budget is less formal and more simplified than the statement of cash flows. As with most other managerial accounting tools, the cash budget is intended for internal use, and is not beholden to the regulatory standards that govern the formatting of formal financial statements, such as the statement of cash flows. Take, for instance, the statement of cash flows for Kathi's business:

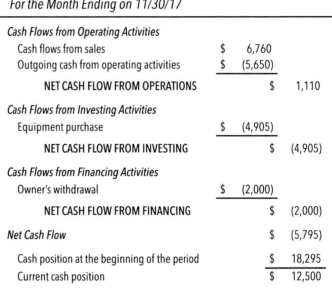

KATHI'S JEWELRY DESIGN
Statement of Cash Flows
For the Month Ending on 11/30/17

Cash Flows from Operating Activities		
Cash flows from sales	$ 6,760	
Outgoing cash from operating activities	$ (5,650)	
NET CASH FLOW FROM OPERATIONS		$ 1,110
Cash Flows from Investing Activities		
Equipment purchase	$ (4,905)	
NET CASH FLOW FROM INVESTING		$ (4,905)
Cash Flows from Financing Activities		
Owner's withdrawal	$ (2,000)	
NET CASH FLOW FROM FINANCING		$ (2,000)
Net Cash Flow		$ (5,795)
Cash position at the beginning of the period		$ 18,295
Current cash position		$ 12,500

Kathi's cash budget has the luxury of being more simple and straightforward (figure 76).

If a business chose to format its cash budget similarly to its statement of cash flows for managerial accounting purposes, it certainly could do that, but most businesses opt for a simpler format.

NOTE

Financial budgets are known in the industry as "pro forma financial statements." Pro forma financial statements are essentially any statements that rely on projections and assumptions, not just budgets. For instance, a business that is considering two or three different expansion strategies may draw up a few pro forma financial statements in order to visualize where either option would lead the business financially.

GRAPHIC

fig. 76

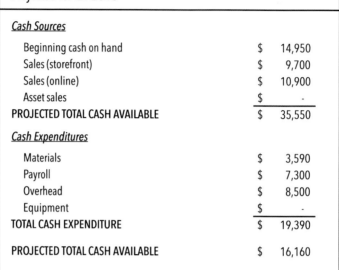

KATHI'S JEWLERY DESIGN
Cash Budget
Projected for Q1 2018

Cash Sources		
Beginning cash on hand	$	14,950
Sales (storefront)	$	9,700
Sales (online)	$	10,900
Asset sales	$	-
PROJECTED TOTAL CASH AVAILABLE	$	35,550
Cash Expenditures		
Materials	$	3,590
Payroll	$	7,300
Overhead	$	8,500
Equipment	$	-
TOTAL CASH EXPENDITURE	$	19,390
PROJECTED TOTAL CASH AVAILABLE	$	16,160

Businesses that regularly make significant investments may choose to keep separate investing budgets, such as the "capital expenditure budget," which is usually devoted to spending on capital assets and long-term projects. In larger organizations, the capital expenditure budget and other investment budgets can span several years. For instance, real estate development companies are constantly on the hunt for land-buying opportunities and are likely to keep investment budgets to track their anticipated spending on land over the next several years.

REMEMBER

In budgeting and throughout managerial accounting, businesses are free to choose, customize, and modify their accounting strategy and accounting tools in response to their industry and their changing needs.

Other budget types include (but are not limited to) the following:

» **The Program Budget** – A large corporate retail chain is shocked by a company-wide PR report showing that four out of ten customers feel they received average to below-average service during their shopping experience. The business decides to implement a sweeping, aggressive new training program to improve the quality of its personnel. The expense of this program might be tracked using a program budget, which is simply a budget that is applied to a specific program or initiative undertaken by a business.

» **The Strategic Budget** – The strategic budget (or "strategic budgeting") is used when various business strategy implementations, such as restructuring, the introduction of a new product line, a major expansion, or other events create a need for a longer-term budget, one that spans more than just a year's time. Strategic budgets are used to monitor and fulfill business endeavors that will improve the business's strategic position over the long term.

» **The Add-On Budget** – In many situations it is not necessary to make any changes to a budget quarter-by-quarter or even year-by-year. An "add-on budget" is created by using the previous term's budget as a template and modifying it only so as to keep it current with the times. An add-on budget may make adjustments for things like inflation, changing wage rates, or new regulatory requirements, but it is essentially the same budget as the one from the previous term.

Budgeting Software for Consideration

Below is a list of some of the best-selling budgeting software for small to medium businesses.[10]

» **Budget Maestro**
This software is designed to help with budgeting, forecasting, financial consolidation, performance analysis and reporting processes. Reviewers say it works for a wide variety of industries, is easy to use, and, when combined with companion products such as Link Maestro and Analytics Maestro, it can help ensure that the budgets you create are based on current and realistic data.

» **PlanGuru**
This one includes features that assist with budgeting, forecasting, and even performance review. PlanGuru prides itself on its simple setup, its import features, and its twenty different forecasting methods, which are customizable to different kinds of businesses. However, it was built for accountants, so it may be a little complicated for those lacking in extensive accounting experience.

> » **Quicken Home and Business**
> Quicken is one of the most well-known brands in this space, and this particular software has so many potential applications. Great for sole proprietorships and S corporations, it offers tools for budgeting monthly expenses and forecasting for the upcoming year. It is inexpensive and can be learned in a relatively short amount of time.

> » **Palo Alto Software Business Plan Pro**
> This planning and budgeting software is designed specifically for those launching new businesses. It offers development tools that can be used to create business plans and budgets that can be presented to bankers and other potential investors. Professional-looking charts, graphs, and reports can be printed at the touch of a button, and the company is famous for its excellent support team.

More on Managerial Accounting

Given its industry-by-industry peculiarities and overall lack of standardization, managerial accounting is an incredibly broad topic, too broad to sufficiently cover in a single academic textbook, much less a single chapter in a beginner-level guide to accounting.

Here are a few other managerial accounting concepts you may come across during your larger accounting study.

> » **Standard costing** – Standard costing is a managerial accounting technique that relies on estimated rather than actual costs for products and services. Estimated costs based on projections or historical data are used initially to track cost of goods sold, gross profit, etc. These estimates are periodically scrutinized and revised via the calculation of "variances." If a product is found to have more cost than previously estimated, then the variance identified is considered an "unfavorable" variance. If the product is found to have less cost, then the variance is "favorable."

> » **Normal costing** – As opposed to relying on estimates and projections, normal costing strives to calculate the actual material, labor, and overhead costs associated with production or service delivery. Like standard costing, normal costing is also subject to variances in the event that actual costs are found to differ from those which were assumed. In both normal and standard costing, when small variances are found, only the costs of goods sold will need to

be adjusted. When large variances are found, the inventory accounts must be adjusted as well.

» **Activity-based costing** – Sometimes referred to as "ABC," activity-based costing is the notion in managerial accounting that all overhead expense is *not* equal. Activity-based costing forces businesses, particularly manufacturing businesses, to assess factors other than machine hours and direct labor hours when determining the cost of a product. For example, a filter-manufacturing company may produce over the course of a year hundreds of thousands of basic mass-produced filters and a couple thousand specialty filters. While the two products may appear to have the same cost in terms of machine and labor hours, activity-based costing would require the company to acknowledge that the specialty filters incur added costs in the form of changes to the production line, consulting time spent with the client in need of a specialty filter, and other activities.

» **Job order costing** – A construction company that builds homes may choose to track its costs according to job order. Rather than track all lumber expense in a big-bucket lumber expense category, job order costing demands that house A's lumber expense be distinguishable from house B's. Law firms and accounting firms are other examples of businesses inclined to track a distinct set of costs on a client-by-client basis. The billable hours spent doing legal research for client A must be separated from the billable hours spent doing research for client B.

» **Work in process accounting** – A manufacturing business will maintain inventory accounts to track both raw materials and finished products ready for sale. In some manufacturing operations there is a significant intermediary period between the initial processing of raw materials and the creation of a complete product. Products in various stages of completion are known as works in process or (WIPs). WIP accounting involves the integration of WIPs into the business's inventory accounts for the purpose of maintaining accurate inventory valuations, financial records, etc.

» **Make or buy analysis** – A make or buy analysis involves the decision of a business to either outsource or produce/deliver a product/service in-house. Naturally, costs are a huge factor in make or buy analyses, but so are control, strategy, and even negotiation opportunities.

A massive retailer/manufacturer, such as Walmart or Costco, may pressure wholesalers into lowering their prices on the grounds that it would be more profitable for the retailer to make certain products on its own rather than purchase from an outside vendor.

In addition to the study of classic managerial accounting principles and tactics, those interested in developing the managerial accountant skillset should prepare to be creative. Business by business, department by department, and even year by year, new opportunities for innovative managerial accounting solutions present themselves. Effective and highly sought-after managerial accountants will know how to leverage their academic knowledge and professional experience into high-impact, form-fitting, difference-making solutions.

Chapter Recap

» Managerial accounting is the application of accounting principles for internal use by business decision-makers.

» A business's ability to control costs and turn profits with utmost efficiency can be enhanced through the application of cost-volume-profit analysis (CVP).

» The "break-even point" in any given accounting period is the point at which enough sales revenue is earned to pay for all variable and fixed costs.

» Contribution margin measures the extent to which the sale of a given product or group of products contributes to paying the business's fixed expenses.

» The wholesale price of inventory purchased by a business for resale is usually debited into an inventory (asset account) and then gradually credited out of the account and moved into cost of goods sold as the inventory is sold off to customers.

» A business's master budget is composed of several smaller budgets that help the business account for its operating, financing, and investing activities.

| 7 |
Monitoring Stocks & Investments

Chapter Overview
> » Understanding GAAP
> » The House of GAAP
> » Evaluating Investments
> » Sustainable Income
> » Financial Reports

Accounting was the course that helped me more than anything.
— JULIAN ROBERTSON, aka The Wizard of Wall Street

In the previous chapter we approached accounting from the perspective of a small business owner. In this chapter we will approach accounting from the perspective of an outside investor, someone who is interested in buying into a business, property, or other asset, but is not necessarily interested in participating in its day-by-day management. In this chapter we will assume that investment decisions are driven by cold, unbiased financial analysis, not by personal networks or passion projects.

The purpose of this chapter is to provide an overview of the ways in which financial accounting is used to support investment decision-making. It is not intended to be used as a comprehensive or instructive resource that can be exclusively relied on for investment guidance.

We will begin this chapter with a discussion of GAAP, the Generally Accepted Accounting Principles. GAAP helps to ensure that accountants use similar, comparable approaches and definitions when producing financial statements and other accounting data. We will discuss GAAP first because it establishes the rules of the playing field when it comes to how financial data is recorded and reported.

What Is GAAP and Why Does It Matter?
Companies that are publicly traded (meaning anyone can buy shares) must provide the market with a way to compare their financial credentials with

those of other companies also competing for investor dollars. The methods and assumptions used by companies when disclosing their financial credentials must be uniform. If, for example, one company were permitted to broaden its definition of "income" and narrow its definition of "expense," then it could produce income statements that would not fairly compare with the income statements of other companies that chose more strict definitions for income and expense. Investors have a reasonable expectation that their investment decisions will be made on the basis of apples-to-apples comparisons.

Furthermore, standardization in financial reporting is important for tax purposes. Imagine if IRS auditors were required to spend valuable time and energy on the taxpayer's dime learning the unique, quirky accounting methods of every business.

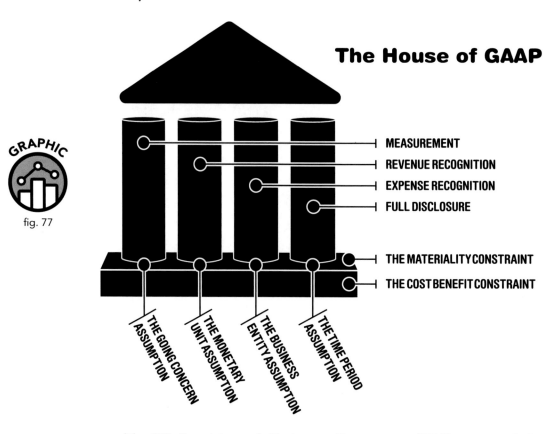

GRAPHIC

fig. 77

The House of GAAP

- MEASUREMENT
- REVENUE RECOGNITION
- EXPENSE RECOGNITION
- FULL DISCLOSURE

- THE MATERIALITY CONSTRAINT
- THE COST BENEFIT CONSTRAINT

THE GOING CONCERN ASSUMPTION

THE MONETARY UNIT ASSUMPTION

THE BUSINESS ENTITY ASSUMPTION

THE TIME PERIOD ASSUMPTION

The US Securities and Exchange Commission (SEC) instituted the GAAP system of rules to make sure accounting methods are somewhat uniform throughout the country. As mentioned in chapter 1, GAAP stands for the Generally Accepted Accounting Principles. The purpose of GAAP is to advance a body of clear, fair, and optimal principles that all businesses are expected to follow. In addition to protecting stockholders and stock traders who need a clear way of comparing various businesses side-by-side, standardization through GAAP is good for accountants as well. If you are competent in financial accounting in accordance with GAAP standards, then you are in some sense eminently hirable throughout the country. When every business is expected to abide by the same standards, every business has the same needs.

Smaller businesses do not need to worry about highly specific GAAP principles, but should adhere closely to the broader principles governing good accounting practice. The owner or manager of a smaller business should understand what is commonly referred to as "The House of GAAP," which is built on four principles (the columns in figure 77), four assumptions (the base of the house upon which the columns/principles rest), and the two accounting constraints (the foundation of the house, which, was it not stable and amenable, would cast the entire structure asunder).

The Four Accounting Principles

1. **The Measurement Principle**
   There are two measurement principles generally used by GAAP. The first is known as the "historical cost principle," which dictates that the value of assets must be recorded in accordance with their historical cost. If a professional farmer buys a tractor for his business—the sticker price is $13,000 but the farmer negotiates the price down to $12,000— the farmer *must always* record the value of the asset as $12,000. Under no circumstances would he record the $13,000 sticker price. Similarly, if a house is purchased for $100,000 and appreciates in value to $110,000, according to the historical cost principle it must still be reported as a $100,000 asset. The second commonly used measurement principle is known as the "fair value principle." This measurement principle can be applied to assets that have a readily identifiable price tag at any given moment. The value of stocks, for instance, is often reported using the fair value principle, because their fair market price is usually readily accessible.

NOTE

The measurement principle does, of course, allow for adjustments to the value of assets purchased in accordance with accepted standards of depreciation. When assets depreciate, the estimated amount of the depreciation can be written off as an expense. However, if an asset such as land, real estate, or other tangible property is purchased at a certain price and *appreciates* in value, then the recorded value of the asset is not generally increased but reported in accordance with the historical cost of the purchase.

2. **The Revenue Recognition Principle**

   With this principle, the GAAP clearly asserts itself as an accrual-based accounting methodology rather than a cash-based methodology. The revenue recognition principle holds that revenue is recognized (accounted for) at the point at which it is earned, not necessarily at the point at which it is paid. Imagine you are the owner of a mental health support conglomerate. Collectively, you have billed for 150 hours of client sessions and you have dispatched $120,000 worth of invoices, but only $60,000 has been paid. According to GAAP, you must still report $120,000 in revenue.

NOTE

Technically speaking, you would report the $60,000 that has been paid in your cash account and the remaining $60,000 in your accounts receivable account. Assuming, however, that some of your clients are simply never going to pay you for your services, which is a factor many businesses must face, you would depreciate the $60,000 in accounts receivable by crediting the amount you are not likely to ever receive, and then making an equal debit on the equity side in a specialized expense account that you can call "nonpayment expense." From that point forward, you will always be able to assess how much your company's net income is suffering due to non-paying clients.

   Simply put, in accordance with GAAP's revenue recognition principle, the proceeds from selling products and services need not always be in cash, but can also take other forms, such as a promise to pay (credit).[11] A business's revenues can be accounted for both by the quantity of cash it receives and by the value of any other assets that are obtained through the sale of goods and services.

3. **The Expense Recognition Principle**

   This principle holds that a business is always required to report expenses within the same accounting period as related revenues. The expense recognition principle is related to another important concept in accounting known as the *"matching principle,"* which says that expenses must be matched (on the same statement) as the revenues that they helped procure. Through adherence to the matching principle, income statements are made more coherent, because reported expenses and revenues are relevant to one another. As you know, both expense and revenue accounts are equity accounts, and total revenues minus total expenses generate a business's net income.

4. **The Full Disclosure Principle**

   According to the full disclosure principle, businesses must always report in detail items on a financial report that would impact the users of the report. For example, if your small business was applying for a bank loan, and you knew that the business was soon to be subject to a significant rent increase (or any other significant financial change), then, for the sake of transparency, you would need to report that detail on the financial statement submitted to the loan officer.

Full disclosure items are often added to the end of financial reports as footnotes.

The Four Accounting Assumptions

1. **The Going Concern Assumption**

   This assumption holds that a business is going to continue to operate and will not be sold or closed. A business that is in the process of liquidating its assets and closing up shop (or a business that is soon to be sold off) will be valued differently than a business that is a going concern, and it behooves the business to be transparent on this matter.

2. **The Monetary Unit Assumption**

   This assumption holds that accounting records are always reported using monetary values, such as US dollars. Depending on the country in which the business operates, different monetary values may be used. It is also, at times, necessary for reports to be issued in different versions for different currencies.

3. **The Business Entity Assumption**

   This assumption emphasizes the importance of treating the business as an independent entity rather than merely as an extension of the business owner(s). A lot of small business owners get into hot water thinking they can blur the line between themselves and their businesses. The business entity assumption demands that business owners and managers treat business finances (revenues, expenses) separately from personal finances.

4. **The Time Period Assumption**

   This assumption holds that a company's functioning is divided into specific time periods—months, years, fiscal years—and that reports can be devised to intelligently comment upon this periodic financial activity.

The Two Accounting Constraints:

1. **The Materiality Constraint**
    Have you ever watched a courtroom drama and heard an attorney say, "It's immaterial!" The materiality constraint says that businesses need only record and report information that has the potential to influence the decisions of a reasonable person. In other words, if you buy an extra pen at the office supply store before going into a meeting and you neglect to save the receipt or file and report it as an expense, then you are probably not going to end up in jail. The transaction was immaterial.

2. **The Cost Benefit Constraint**
    This simple constraint holds that disclosures are only necessary when their benefits outweigh the costs of producing them. In other words, the cost incurred during the process of providing financial statements should be measured against the benefits garnered by the users of that information. If the information is determined to be negligible, then it may be left out of the financial statements. It is occasionally difficult for smaller businesses to quantify the benefits associated with said information, which makes this constraint confusing at times. In larger companies, it is generally easier to determine whether investors, creditors, etc. will benefit from various types of information access.

Investor Focal Points

Now that you have a clearer understanding of the underlying principles, assumptions, and constraints that serve to equalize public-facing financial data, we may begin to consider what exactly it is that investors are looking for when assessing the financial well-being of a business.

Perhaps the most essential quality of a business is its ability to generate income. GAAP helps to ensure that a business's net income is reported fairly and accurately from period to period. But investors assess income from a multitude of different vantage points. Not only are they looking for evidence that the company has been able to turn profits, they also look to confirm that the prevalence of a business's income generation is based on normal and sustainable business activities. In a given annual accounting period, twenty million dollars of income generated by a mid-sized record company following the unexpected breakout success of a new jazz album is quite different from twenty million dollars of income generated by an industrial supply company that owes its success to its normal day-to-day operations.

Sustainable income is a term used by investors to describe a business's ability to generate income on a perpetual basis. In our example, the twenty million dollars is more likely to qualify as sustainable income in the case of the industrial supply company.

When companies release their income statements to the public, they usually distinguish the revenues and expenses that are "operational" from other revenues and expenses. This distinction gives investors an ability to gauge which revenue directly relates to the business's normal activities and therefore constitutes sustainable income.

The value of any given company, as determined by investors, is a product of its position in the market, the quantity of its earnings, and the reliability of its earnings. The reliability factor in particular can be assessed through an evaluation of the company's sustainable income.

Annual Reports

The key financial statements discussed in chapters 1 and 2 (income statement, retained earnings statement, balance sheet, statement of cash flow) are disclosed by public companies in an *annual report*, which also includes analysis and notes from the company's management. An independent auditor's report is also included with the annual report so as to add an additional layer of verification and to check the company's compliance with GAAP. The auditor must be a certified public accountant (CPA).

For current and potential investors, the annual report essentially represents the business's sales pitch. The analysis section includes discussions of the various trends that the business is anticipating, both positive and negative, and ideas are presented that elaborate on the business's plans and strategies for facing challenges and maximizing opportunities in the coming years.

Highly trained accountants may also be interested in the notes that accompany the financial statements, detailing the accounting methods used in the creation of the statements. Veteran accountants will appreciate a behind-the-scenes discussion of accounting intricacies.

Pro Forma Income

In an investor's pursuit to identify sustainable income, pro forma income reports are often used, though with a fair degree of caution. *Pro forma income* is a simple concept; it is a secondary (non-GAAP) measurement of income that excludes items that the company deems unusual or nonrecurring. For example, if a company incurs a one-time expense to obtain a license to sell a certain product, it may be required to report that expense in its GAAP-compliant income statement but may opt to omit it from its pro forma report. In fact, many companies have reported pro forma income that varies dramatically from the same company's formal GAAP-compliant reporting, often showing substantially higher income. In an effort to reduce bad-faith reporting of pro forma income, the SEC has issued guidance on pro forma reporting methods.

From an investor's standpoint, pro forma income reports ostensibly provide insight into what the company is capable of generating on an ongoing basis under normal circumstances. The trained accountant has an advantage here, in that she is in a unique position to evaluate the integrity of a given company's pro forma reporting and to determine whether it is mostly hype or an even-keel assessment of the company's income-generating power.

Choosing Investments

From the perspective of a personal investor or a company decision-maker shopping for a place to park surplus cash, strong knowledge of accounting principles can be of use on a variety of fronts. As we have discussed thus far, a familiarization with the ways in which public financial reporting is standardized, particularly through GAAP, is important when assessing the levelness of the playing field. Once the investor is reasonably confident in the accuracy and standardization of reporting, he can proceed with a side-by-side, apples-to-apples evaluation of potential investments.

There are three principal comparison methods by which investments may be evaluated. You may recognize the first two from chapter 3.

1. **Intracompany Basis** – Comparing a company to itself. An intracompany comparison involves assessing a company's performance over previous years against its recent performance and evaluating its future potential.

2. **Intercompany Basis** – Comparing like companies. Intercompany comparisons involve evaluating income statements, balance sheets, etc. company by company, accounting period by accounting period. Intercompany comparisons are most relevant when companies hail from the same industrial sector. Compare large chemical companies to other large chemical companies. Compare mid-size motor manufacturing companies to other mid-size motor manufacturing companies.

3. **Industry Average** – Comparing a company to the industry average. Industry average comparisons involve evaluating the performance of a company from a specific industry and comparing that company's financial performance with that of the industry's average performance.

Ratios

When choosing investments, investors study various ratios that can be derived from financial statements and compared to one another using the three comparison methods mentioned above. Some of the most common ratios you are likely to come across when evaluating investment include the following:

The Current Ratio

fig. 78

$$\text{CURRENT RATIO} = \frac{\text{CURRENT ASSETS}}{\text{CURRENT LIABILITIES}}$$

The current ratio, introduced in chapter 3, is one of several liquidity ratios. As with most liquidity ratios, its main purpose is to assess the extent to which the company is capable of handling its current debt load.

Current assets and current liabilities should be clearly delineated on a company's balance sheet. "Current assets" refer to assets that can be readily converted into cash within a year's time. Similarly, "current liabilities" are liabilities (debt) that are expected to be resolved (paid off) within a year's time.

A good current ratio should assure you that the company's short-term debt can be readily paid off by its cash-convertible assets. Ideally, you would prefer that the assets cover the debts at a 2:1 ratio. The minimum current ratio to be found in a healthy company is usually considered 1:1.

The Price-to-Earnings Ratio

fig. 79

$$\text{PRICE TO EARNINGS (P/E) RATIO} = \frac{\text{MARKET CAP}}{\text{TOTAL EARNINGS}} \text{ OR } \frac{\text{SHARE PRICE}}{\text{EARNINGS PER SHARE}}$$

The price-to-earnings or "P/E" ratio is perhaps the most widely used of several solvency ratios. Whereas liquidity ratios gauge a company's ability to attend to its short-term debt, solvency ratios assess a company's ability to survive and prosper in the long term. A high P/E ratio is a signal that the market believes the company is positioned to grow and bring in big earnings in the future, even if its current earnings are not high. A low P/E ratio, though not a sign of explosive growth potential, may be a good buying signal for investors looking for a more steady and reliable return. Generally, low P/E stocks are thought to be "cheap," and high P/E stocks are thought to be "expensive."

A more comprehensive discussion of liquidity and solvency ratios can be found in the *Investing QuickStart Guide: The Simplified Beginner's Guide to Successfully Navigating the Stock Market, Growing Your Wealth & Creating a Secure Financial Future*,[12] also available from ClydeBank Media.

Don't forget to take advantage of the Digital Assets included with your purchase of this book. Among other supplemental material, you will find resources like a digital ratio cheat sheet that contains formulas and analyses of nine different ratios used to assess a business's financial well-being. Access this cheat sheet and all Digital Asset files for this title at: www.clydebankmedia.com/accounting-assets.

Chapter Recap

» GAAP norms and standards help to ensure the uniformity and comparability of financial reporting.

» The core components of GAAP can be summarized in four principles, four assumptions, and two constraints.

» Investors analyze annual reports and pro forma income in an effort to better understand a company's potential.

» When evaluating investments, ratios such as the current ratio and the price-to-earnings ratio may be used to evaluate a company's growth potential and ability to pay its debts.

| 8 |

Income Tax Accounting
Keeping Your Business Out of IRS Crosshairs

Chapter Overview
- » Marginal and Average Tax Rates
- » FIFO and LIFO
- » Tax Deductions and Tax Credits
- » Tax Shelters

The US tax code was written by A students. Every April 15, we have to pay somebody who got an A in accounting to keep ourselves from being sent to jail.

         – P. J. O'ROURKE, political satirist

Good accounting practices can keep a business legally compliant while minimizing its tax burden. From the retail storefront tax professionals who help individuals file their income taxes in April to the accounting firms hired to handle the complex income taxes of Fortune 500 companies, income tax services are representative of an enormous industry. The reality is that most every individual, business, and nonprofit is required to dutifully and accurately file and pay (if they owe) income taxes. The certainty of taxes—of a nature second only to death—ensures that accounting remains a highly stable, high-demand profession.

Even tax-exempt organizations, in most cases, are required to file an "annual information return," which provides information about incoming funds and outgoing expenditures. A charity, for instance, must keep records of how its money is raised and spent, and thus will often require the assistance of a professional accountant.

Income tax accounting refers to the branch of accounting that focuses only on financial events which affect an individual or business's income tax liability. Income tax accounting professionals must be intimately familiar with the current rules and regulations governing income taxes as set forth by the Internal Revenue Service (IRS).

Marginal Tax Rate versus Average Tax Rate

For business owners and entrepreneurs, the tax factor can play an important motivational (or counter-motivational) role in the decision about whether or not to pursue additional revenue and, if yes, how aggressively. At any given moment in the life of a business, the next dollar earned will be subject to a particular taxation rate, something known as the "marginal tax rate." The marginal tax rate will usually not remain the same throughout the life of the business, or even throughout the duration of any given year. The marginal tax rate changes based on how much income the business has taken in over the course of the year (or fiscal year). A business may be able to earn $5,000 tax-free, a marginal tax rate of 0 percent. The next $5,000 earned may be taxed at 15 percent. Once the business has $10,000 in income, the next $5,000 might be taxed at a marginal tax rate of 20 percent. The *marginal tax rate* refers to the rate of taxation currently being exerted against income during the course of a tax year. As an accountant, it is important to know how much gross revenue your client, employer, or business is taking in, but it is equally, if not more, important to know the amount of gross revenue your client, employer, or business is entitled to keep. At the end of the day, before we determine profit, we must take into account the money that will be given up in taxes.

A common misunderstanding about income taxes is that the tax rate for any given income level is applied to every dollar earned by that individual or business during the course of the tax year. In reality, even though an individual or business may earn enough to enter into a higher tax bracket, the money they earn at lower brackets is not retroactively affected.

fig. 80

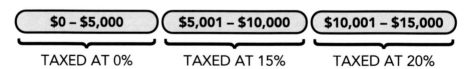

| $0 – $5,000 | $5,001 – $10,000 | $10,001 – $15,000 |
| TAXED AT 0% | TAXED AT 15% | TAXED AT 20% |

Based on the marginal tax rates depicted in figure 80, even if the individual or business earns over $10,000 and crosses into the 20 percent marginal tax rate, the initial $5,000 earned is still taxed at 0 percent and the next $5,000 is still taxed at 15 percent. Marginal rates are not retroactive.

Even though money earned at a certain tax rate cannot be retroactively taxed at a different rate, the "average tax rate" of an individual or business does increase as more money is made. The ***average tax rate*** is calculated by determining how much tax is owed relative to total income. Using our brackets from figure 80, assume that a business earns $13,000 in taxable income; $5,000 is taxed at 0 percent ($0), $5,000 is taxed at 15 percent ($750), and $3,000 is taxed at 20 percent ($600). The business would pay a total of $1,350 in taxes, which is 10.4 percent of total income. The average tax rate is therefore 10.4 percent.

The more money you earn that is taxed at a higher rate, the higher your average tax rate will become. But as a matter of fact, the income you make early in the year (or fiscal year) will likely be taxed at a lower rate than the income you make later in the year. This system of gradually increasing marginal tax rates is known as a progressive tax system. All income tax systems throughout the world are progressive in nature. In theory, the progressive tax system protects individuals from losing the income that they desperately need. For instance, consider someone who only earns $5,000 a year. It is more likely that he will need to use every penny of his income than it is likely for an earner of $5,000,000 to need every penny of his income.

The opposite of a progressive tax system is a regressive tax system, in which the less money made, the greater the bite taken out by the tax man. The sales tax, for instance, is a regressive tax. If our individual making $5,000 purchases $2,500 worth of goods and the sales tax is 10 percent, then he pays $250 in tax. If our individual making $5,000,000 purchases the same amount of goods at the same rate, he also pays $250 in sales tax. For the $5,000 earner, this $250 tax is 5 percent of his entire income. For the $5,000,000 earner, the $250 tax is only a miniscule one eighth of a percent of his entire income.

Accrual versus Cash Basis Accounting for Income Tax Purposes

Businesses that have earned over $10 million annually in gross revenue over the previous three years (on average) are required by the IRS to use accrual basis accounting when filing their taxes. Businesses that average under $10 million may use either accrual or cash basis.

The cash basis is usually the preferred choice for small businesses, most of which, in my experience, tend to prefer using cash basis for both their income tax and their general accounting needs. When opting for the cash basis for income tax purposes, all cash entering the business before the close of the year (or fiscal year) is taxable. Expenses incurred by the business can only be written off if they have been paid. When the business elects (or is required) to use accrual basis accounting for income tax purposes, expenses may be written off even if they have not been paid, and accrued revenues are all taxable, even if the cash has yet to be collected from clients/customers; tax liability is incurred as soon as a service has been performed or a good delivered.

Generally, businesses that keep inventories, even if they average less than $10 million in annual revenue, are required to use the accrual basis to account for their inventory. These businesses may use cash accounting when deducting their other expenses, but the IRS requires that inventory expense remain closely aligned with revenue received for the sale of said inventory. The optimal practice, for tax and general purposes, is to deduct inventory expense as inventory is sold, resulting in an instantaneous and accurate net revenue adjustment.

Businesses are allowed some flexibility when it comes to whether they use the first-in first-out (FIFO) or last- in first-out (LIFO) method when accounting for inventory. **FIFO** requires that the assumed cost of goods sold for a given product is the cost of the product that has been in inventory the longest.

If a tire retailer purchases 1,000 tires at a cost of $40 per tire, and then a month later purchases another 1,000 tires (the same kind) for $42 per unit, then, with FIFO accounting, the cost of goods sold for the first 1,000 tires will be $40 per tire. Under **LIFO**, as soon as the second batch of tires was purchased, the cost of goods sold for the next 1,000 tire sales would be $42.

fig. 81

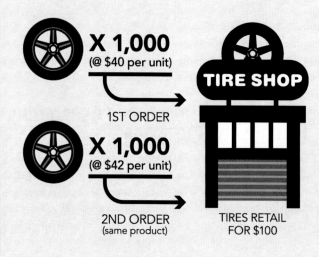

X 1,000
(@ $40 per unit)

1ST ORDER

X 1,000
(@ $42 per unit)

2ND ORDER
(same product)

TIRE SHOP

TIRES RETAIL
FOR $100

OPTION A:
The business uses **FIFO.**

The cost per tire is recorded as $40 per unit. After the first 1,000 units sell, the cost recorded is $42 per unit.

OPTION B:
The business uses **LIFO.**

The cost per tire is recorded as $42 per unit. After the first 1,000 units sell, the cost recorded is $40 per unit.

For tax purposes, businesses may use the LIFO method, which, if inflation is on the rise, will reduce net profit and will therefore reduce taxable income. Companies that use LIFO for tax purposes are still free to use FIFO for their formal public-facing financial statements and, of course, are free to use any system they prefer for their managerial accounting endeavors.

The rules and regulations governing income taxes and those governing formal financial reporting stem from two different authorities. The IRS is the source for rules governing income tax filing, and GAAP (chapter 7) is the source for rules governing the proper preparation of formal financial statements.

Tax Deductions and Tax Credits

It is important to understand the difference between a tax deduction and a tax credit. A tax deduction reduces taxable income, whereas a tax credit directly reduces the amount of tax owed.

Recall our sample marginal tax rates from figure 80.

$0 – $5,000	$5,001 – $10,000	$10,001 – $15,000
TAXED AT 0%	TAXED AT 15%	TAXED AT 20%

If a shoeshine business earns $9,000 under these rates, the first $5,000 is taxed at 0 percent and the next $4,000 will be taxed at 15 percent, culminating in a total tax liability of $600. **Tax deductions** allow businesses (and individuals) to reduce their total amount of taxable earnings. For instance, if the shoeshine business qualifies for a $1,000 tax deduction, then its taxable income will be reduced from $9,000 to $8,000, and it will owe $450 in tax rather than $600.

Tax deductions for businesses come in the form of normal business expenses; for example, supplies, advertising, rent, and payments made for professional services, such as accounting. These deductible expenditures also include contributions made by employers to employee benefit plans (health, dental, vision, etc.) as well as contributions made to employee retirement plans.

In some circumstances it is possible for individual taxpayers to take tax deductions for their personal contributions to their health insurance and retirement plans. Individuals also commonly deduct interest paid on their home mortgages, paid property taxes, charitable giving, and several other expenditures that the government elects not to tax.

I have come across many individuals over the years, clients and others, who are under the mistaken impression that "tax deductible" somehow equates to "ultimately free." They are often led to believe that their tax deductible investment or expense or gift will ultimately equate to a dollar-for-dollar reduction to their tax bill. If you, by this point, have a proper understanding of what is meant by "tax deduction," then you know it is not a dollar-for-dollar rebate of any kind, but a simple reduction in an individual or business's taxable income. Less income means less tax owed, but in almost all cases, a tax deductible purchase still results in more money spent than saved at tax time.

Tax Deductible ≠ Free

Some types of spending, however, are so highly sought-after by the government that a **tax credit** is offered to negate the taxpayers' total liability. Unlike the tax deduction, a tax credit *is* a direct, dollar-for-dollar reduction in tax burden. If our shoeshine business received a $500 tax credit as opposed to a $1,000 tax deduction, then its tax bill would be reduced from $600 to $100. If you will recall, the $1,000 tax deduction only reduced the tax bill to $450. A tax credit is thought to be the more enticing incentive since it entails a direct reduction of the total tax bill.

Tax credits are awarded to businesses for various reasons, usually to encourage private-sector spending that the government deems highly desirable. Tax credits are subject to changing on a year-by-year basis, but below are some of the most common:

» Tax credits for businesses or individuals who invest in solar or other renewable energy technologies

» Tax credits for start-up businesses that invest in a qualified retirement plan

» Tax credits for small businesses that pay at least half the cost of their employees' health insurance

» Tax credits for small businesses' investments that go toward making their business sites handicap-accessible for employees and customers

» Tax credits for businesses of all sizes that pursue certain types of research and development

A good income tax accountant will stay current on available tax deductions and credits offered by the IRS to ensure that their clients' tax burdens are minimized.

Long-Term Capital Gains versus Ordinary Income

Tax shelters are not just for corporate barons who want to park their cash on the Cayman Islands. There are many straightforward and perfectly legal tax sheltering opportunities available to individuals and businesses looking to lower their tax bills. For instance, one of the most well-known and widely used tax shelters is the retirement savings plan. Individuals and businesses with employees can lower their tax liabilities by participating in qualifying retirement plans.

Another commonly used form of tax shelter is the conversion of ordinary income into long-term capital gains income. The latter is taxed at much lower rates than the former. As you may recall from chapter 1, capital gains income is income derived from the resale of an investment at a higher price than that which was originally paid. When a dividend is received or a stock, bond, or other financial security is sold for a profit, it is considered a capital gain. Only *long-term* capital gains are subject to the lower rate. In order to qualify as long-term, the investment must have been held for at least a year.

Ordinary income, as the name implies, comes from ordinary day-to-day labors. Wages, salaries, tips, commissions, and bonuses all constitute ordinary income.

Crafty accountants may use methods such as the sale of depreciable equipment, the sale of real estate, long-term capital loss carryovers, and a variety of other maneuvers to legally convert ordinary income into capital gains income. It is in the interest of spurring economic investment that long-term capital gains income is taxed at a much lower rate than ordinary income. Even though the capital gains earnings are not based on the earner's actual labor, the government places value on capital investment, because it expands the economy and creates new jobs. The lower capital gains tax rate is meant to cheer on capital investment.

GRAPHIC

fig. 82

TAXABLE INCOME UP TO THIS LEVEL		TAX RATE*	
SINGLE	MARRIED FILING JOINTLY	ORDINARY INCOME MARGINAL TAX RATE (includes short-term capital gains and interest income)	APPROX. LONG-TERM CAPITAL GAINS RATE**
$9,525	$19,050	10%	0%
$38,700	$77,400	12%	0%
$82,500	$165,000	22%	15%
$157,500	$315,000	24%	15%
$200,000	$400,000	32%	15%
$500,000	$600,000	35%	20%
ABOVE	ABOVE	37%	20%

* The rates featured in this graphic are based on those established in the Tax Cuts and Jobs Act of 2017.
** The capital gains rates correspond approximately to the income brackets on the left.

Whether or not the lower capital gains tax rate costs more revenue than it creates in economic value is a matter of much dispute, but one thing is for sure: the disparity in tax rates between normal income and long-term capital gains income has created a kind of cottage industry, one that is manned by armies of accountants always on the hunt for new ways to convert ordinary income into capital gains income.

Figure 82 details the disparity between ordinary income tax rates and long-term capital gains rates.

Why Business Entity Type Matters

In chapter 1 we discussed the main business entity types, like sole proprietorship, partnership, LLC, etc. Entity type has a considerable effect on how a business is taxed. As with many phenomena in accounting, there is a lot of "it depends" when it comes to assessing which business entity type is optimal for any given business.

Many of the small business clients I work with find the concept of "pass-through" taxation somewhat difficult to grasp. If someone sets up an LLC—let's assume for the sake of simplicity that it is a single-owner LLC—and the owner earns $100,000 in profit from the business, those earnings must be taxed. With a single-member LLC (as is also true with multi-member LLCs, S corps, sole proprietorships, and partnerships), the business entity itself is not directly taxed. The profits earned must be claimed by the owner of the LLC; the profits *pass through* the business and are added to the individual owner's personal income tax liability.

The C corporation is the only entity type that is directly taxed at the *entity* level. When a C corporation earns $100,000 in net income, the corporation pays a corporate tax (at a rate that is usually much lower than the personal income tax rate), but once profits are distributed to shareholders in the form of dividends, these earnings are also taxable. It is a phenomenon known as "double taxation."

The following graphic depicts how three businesses, an LLC, an S corporation, and a C corporation, each with $100,000 in net income (revenue minus expenses), may be taxed at the federal level according to 2018 tax rates.

At the time of this writing, sweeping new revisions to the tax code have been passed into law in the form of the Tax Cuts and Jobs Act. Comprehensive tax legislation at the federal level is not a frequent occurrence. The data depicted and modeled in figure 82 and figure 83, respectively, are reflective of current tax realities in the aftermath of this legislation.

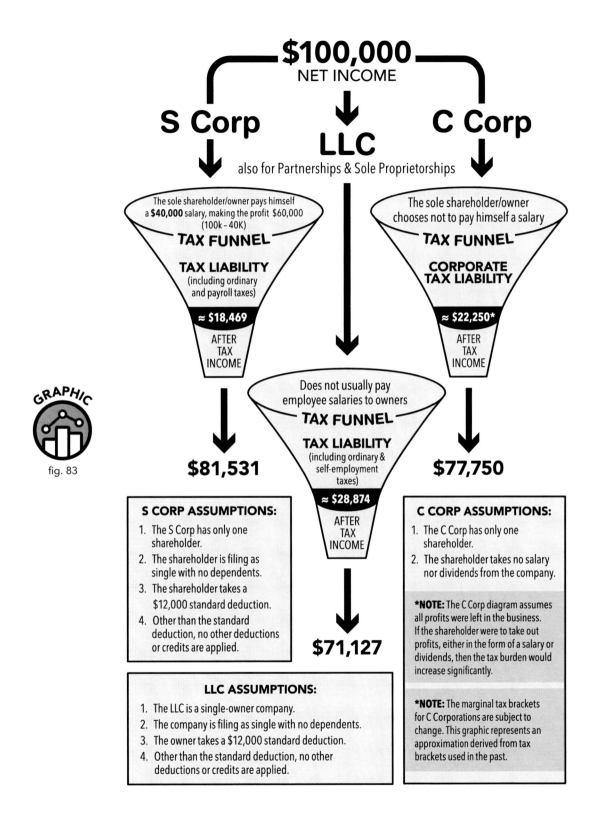

$100,000
NET INCOME

S Corp

LLC
also for Partnerships & Sole Proprietorships

C Corp

The sole shareholder/owner pays himself a **$40,000** salary, making the profit $60,000 (100k – 40K)
TAX FUNNEL

TAX LIABILITY
(including ordinary and payroll taxes)

≈ **$18,469**

AFTER TAX INCOME

The sole shareholder/owner chooses not to pay himself a salary
TAX FUNNEL

CORPORATE TAX LIABILITY

≈ **$22,250***

AFTER TAX INCOME

Does not usually pay employee salaries to owners
TAX FUNNEL

TAX LIABILITY
(including ordinary & self-employment taxes)

≈ **$28,874**

AFTER TAX INCOME

$81,531

$77,750

$71,127

GRAPHIC
fig. 83

S CORP ASSUMPTIONS:

1. The S Corp has only one shareholder.
2. The shareholder is filing as single with no dependents.
3. The shareholder takes a $12,000 standard deduction.
4. Other than the standard deduction, no other deductions or credits are applied.

C CORP ASSUMPTIONS:

1. The C Corp has only one shareholder.
2. The shareholder takes no salary nor dividends from the company.

*NOTE: The C Corp diagram assumes all profits were left in the business. If the shareholder were to take out profits, either in the form of a salary or dividends, then the tax burden would increase significantly.

*NOTE: The marginal tax brackets for C Corporations are subject to change. This graphic represents an approximation derived from tax brackets used in the past.

LLC ASSUMPTIONS:

1. The LLC is a single-owner company.
2. The company is filing as single with no dependents.
3. The owner takes a $12,000 standard deduction.
4. Other than the standard deduction, no other deductions or credits are applied.

Here are a couple of important things to note about figure 83:

» The S corp and LLC, along with sole proprietorship and partnership, are all "pass-through entities," meaning all company profits (including dividends from the S corp) are divided among the shareholders/owners and are subject to personal income tax. The C corp is not pass-through but is taxed as an independent entity. Distributed company profits (dividends) are then taxed *again* at the shareholder level as capital gains (double taxation).

» The first two funnels, S corp and LLC, assume that the shareholder/owner is deriving personal income from the company, either in the form of salary, dividends, capital gains or some combination thereof. The third funnel, C corp, assumes all profits are retained by the company. This is why the after-tax income of the C corp appears to be the highest of the three. If the C corp shareholder took a salary from the company (taxable) and/or dividend payments (also taxable), then the after-tax income would likely be the *lowest* of the three.

» The marginal tax brackets for C corporations are subject to change. Figure 83 represents an approximation derived from tax brackets used in the past.

More on Taxes

Like managerial accounting, income tax accounting is a vast subject and certainly worthy of its own book. In fact, I've written a book on taxes that I think you would find useful. It is called *Taxes for Small Businesses QuickStart Guide* and is available through ClydeBankMedia.com. Check it out!

Chapter Recap

» Income tax systems throughout the world use a marginal tax rate, where higher levels of earnings are progressively taxed at higher rates.

» The average tax rate can be calculated by dividing total tax paid by total taxable income.

» Businesses may file their taxes using the cash basis method only if their revenues are under $10 million annually.

» Tax deductions reduce taxable income, and tax credits directly reduce total tax assessed.

» The conversion of ordinary income into long-term capital gains income is one of the most popular forms of tax sheltering.

| 9 |
Detecting and Preventing Fraud

Chapter Overview
» Factors Contributing to Workplace Fraud
» Preventing Fraud
» Cash Control Systems
» Bank Statement Reconciliation

Ethics and fraud prevention are critical aspects of accounting. Accountants and bookkeepers, as well as any business professionals handling sensitive financial records, must exercise an exceptional degree of ethical decision-making and scrutiny. A person with a strong ethical compass may find it difficult to envision the many ways in which fraud can potentially damage a business.

Fraud comes in many flavors and its culprits span all ages, genders, colors, and creeds.

True story: a trainer at a medical insurance company was in charge of training new personnel on how to submit claims to the accounts receivable department for payment. As part of the training, she would send in fake claims with fictitious payees and was responsible for notifying accounts payable so they would not pay out any claims to health care providers that did not exist. Because there was little control exerted by the insurance company over claim submissions, the trainer chose to set up a couple of fake companies, under her control, and to use these fake companies as fictitious payees when training new employees. The trainer intentionally failed to notify the accounts payable department when using her own companies for training purposes. Over time, accounts payable paid out some $11 million to fake companies controlled by the fraudster.

Another true story: a bookkeeper at a construction company was in charge of reconciling bank statements (checking bank records against internal accounting records) and was also a clerk in accounts payable—a dangerous combination of duties from the outset. She defrauded her company by submitting expenses to be paid that were not real expenses. The supervisor would sign the checks, and the fraudster would then white out the payee line of the check and write in the name of an account that she controlled. The end result was $570,000 worth of criminal embezzlement.

There are countless similar stories of fraud affecting companies of all sizes and involving all types of perpetrators. Small-business owners may hold the mistaken impression that their close-knit, family-like work environment makes them immune from fraud. In reality, the centralization of control in many small business environments, and the ensuing difficulty of the small business owner to differentiate job responsibilities and to set up checks and balances, makes small businesses in many ways more vulnerable to fraud, not less.

Ironically, businesses most vulnerable to fraud are those with decision-makers who believe that it cannot happen to them. The proactive implementation of preventative measures is key to reducing the risk of fraud. In this chapter we will review ways in which businesses can assess their risks of fraud and respond appropriately and effectively.

The Fraud Triangle

It is a well-documented fact that the majority of theft comes from within an organization rather than from outside of it.[13] If someone steals a significant quantity of inventory from Kathi's midtown jewelry store in the middle of the night, the odds say that an employee is probably the guilty culprit, as opposed to a random burglar. And what is true for burglary is especially true for embezzlement, which by definition is perpetrated by a person from a position of trust and access.

The fraud triangle, pictured in figure 84, has been used for decades to assess and respond to internal fraud issues.

fig. 84

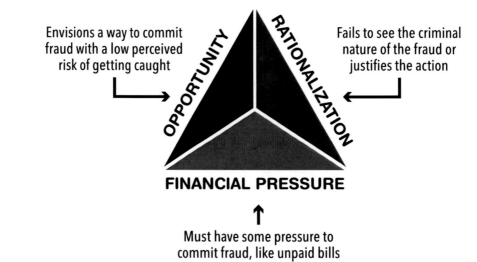

Envisions a way to commit fraud with a low perceived risk of getting caught

Fails to see the criminal nature of the fraud or justifies the action

OPPORTUNITY

RATIONALIZATION

FINANCIAL PRESSURE

Must have some pressure to commit fraud, like unpaid bills

Opportunity

There will always be some individuals who are tempted to steal. It makes no difference whether they have been with you for just a few months or for many years. In order for this temptation to take root, however, the employee must first see an opportunity. Opportunities usually come in the form of missing controls, blind spots in security protocols, or sloppy accounting practices. When a store employee, for example, sees that a manager is not doing regular countdowns of the registers in the store, the employee may see an opportunity to steal money from the register without being detected. In our example from the intro, the trainer at the insurance company saw an opportunity when she realized that any claims she submitted to accounts payable would be paid with no questions asked.

The opportunity side of the triangle is unique in that employees or managers with sufficient personal ethics who see fraud opportunities may be instrumental in implementing preventative actions. Sometimes fraud prevention is about beating the would-be embezzler to the punch. If you take away the opportunity, the rest of the triangle collapses.

As was mentioned previously, smaller businesses do not have the same remedies available to them as larger businesses when it comes to fraud prevention. Larger businesses intentionally diffuse bookkeeping and accounting responsibilities across a large pool of employees and departments to foster a system of checks and balances that inherently minimizes fraud. In small businesses, the owners themselves are often the most important deterrents; they must identify fraud opportunities on their own and take preventative action as needed.

Rationalization

Rationalization can refer to either an inability or unwillingness to see a certain behavior as fraudulent or the willful and personal decision to see something as justified. An example of the former would be a traveling salesman who uses the company credit card to make unauthorized purchases. An example of the latter might be an employee who feels she is being harassed by her boss, and rather than contacting an attorney she decides that she is justified in exploiting an embezzlement opportunity she has identified.

Keep in mind that most individuals do not begin work with a company with plans to defraud the owner as soon as they can identify an opportunity.

Often, it is rationalization that occurs first, followed by the identification of an opportunity. The will to commit fraud is built up over time, often resulting from perceived slights or abuses of the employee by the owner or a manager. A rationalization may occur if an employee feels that he is not being adequately compensated or was passed over for promotion. Since he is not being taken care of by the company, he must take care of himself. And dipping into the company's petty cash account every odd Thursday is not, in his mind, unethical behavior, even though it is.

Financial Pressure

Financial pressure is the third segment of the fraud triangle. It refers to an employee's personal financial circumstances, bills that need to be paid, a sick relative, skyrocketing gambling debt. When he faces enormous financial pressure, he is more likely to succumb to fraud. There are also plenty of cases where the financial pressure was the intense desire of the fraudster to upgrade his or her lifestyle. Couple this materialistic bent with the rationalization that ethics is merely an impendent to the good life, add in the right opportunity, and you've got fraud.

Taking Action to Prevent Fraud

Whether you are the owner of your own business or a low-level accountant for a giant corporation, assessing the three elements of the fraud triangle can help you evaluate fraud risk at your place of business. When "at-risk" employees are identified, your focus should be on preventative measures. It is generally a lot easier and less expensive to prevent fraud from occurring than to detect, prosecute, and account for losses after fraud has been committed.

Here are some actions you can take to minimize fraud risk:

» Use locks and passwords on sensitive records; allow access to sensitive financial information on a need-to-know basis. Use alarms, security monitors, safes, and other physical controls to minimize fraud opportunity.

» Minimize the amount of cash and other liquid inventory items available to employees, especially employees who may be more likely to attempt to defraud the business.

» When it comes to sensitive tasks, such as counting down the cash drawer or making a deposit at the bank, assign clear responsibilities to each employee. Segregate duties whenever possible so that the work of any given employee provides checks on the work of others.

A common practice in businesses of all sizes is to segregate the accountant's duties from the custodian's duties. The accountant, for instance, is in charge of maintaining the books that document the flow of cash and inventories. Other employees (the custodians) should maintain physical control over these assets. If the person keeping the books is the same person who maintains physical control over the assets, then there is fraud opportunity.

» Source documents (chapter 5) should be promptly forwarded to the accounting department to ensure timely recording of transactions.

» Documents issued by the company—checks, invoices, purchase orders, etc.—should be pre-numbered. This helps to ensure that transactions do not get recorded more than once and that no transactions are missed.

» Be aware of being defrauded from the outside through the use of fraudulent checks. Banks these days do not even check signatures anymore, but rely instead on numeric codes and other controls.

» Keep close banking relationships. Your business should have a primary contact point at the bank you use, someone who is familiar with you and your business and can vouch for you if something goes wrong.

» Conduct background checks on prospective employees. Background checks generally come with a reasonable price tag and can help prevent your business from bringing on higher-risk employees.

» Insist on employee vacations. Many scams require constant on-site maintenance. Employee vacations can provide unique oversight opportunities of various job functions where fraud opportunities can be assessed and suspected fraud investigated.

» Regularly rotate employee duties. Not only will you be cross-training your employees and making them more valuable to your organization, but duty rotation also acts as a deterrent to fraud. When employees know that they are not going to be permanently assigned to a particular job detail, they also know that their ability to exploit fraud opportunities is limited.

» Consider bonding your employees. The process of bonding involves taking out an insurance policy on your employees that covers your losses in the event of employee theft. Bonding acts as a significant deterrent, because employees are made aware that the bonding company will aggressively prosecute fraud cases.

» Last, but definitely not least, you have to police yourself. It may be tempting to bend the rules a little here and there on the expense report or conveniently forget to replenish the petty cash drawer after you borrow some funds for a lunch outing. For the small business owner, it may be tempting to write off certain personal expenses as business expenses to reduce your overall tax liability, but doing so can make *you* guilty of fraud. If you take a vacation in Bermuda and you take a couple of business phone calls while soaking up the sun, you may be tempted to think that you now have the option to write off your vacation expenses as business expenses. It is very important that the identity of the business entity be maintained and its boundaries be well defined. If you personally set a tone at your business that emphasizes the importance of integrity and respect for the business, then your employees may be more likely to follow suit.

SMALL BUSINESSES BEWARE: Some of the controls and preventative actions discussed above may prove more difficult for smaller businesses to implement. Segregating and rotating duties among employees, for example, can be challenging when you do not have hundreds of employees to work with. A 2014 study found that businesses with fewer than one hundred employees have a higher risk of employee theft.[14]

Preventing Fraudulent Cash Losses

Business owners and managers must entrust employees with the handling of cash assets. Unfortunately, cash, more so than any other asset, is highly susceptible to fraud. Segregation of duties and other internal controls must be put in place in order to minimize this risk.

In the following example, we will take a look at a typical set-up for the handling of over-the-counter receipts in a retail sales operation that handles a lot of cash on a day-by-day basis. See if you can spot any of the fraud prevention strategies listed in the previous section.

A sales clerk is solely responsible for his own drawer for the duration of his eight-hour shift. Once his shift ends, he counts down the drawer and provides his count total and the cash itself to the store manager. The sales clerk's cash register also generates a secure report, the register tape report, which records information from every sale. Only the shift manager or supervisor (someone other than the sales clerk) can access the register tape report. The supervisor sends the register tape report to the accounting department. In the meantime, the store manager, who receives the actual counted cash from the sales clerk, verifies the sales clerk's count total and enters the amount on a bank deposit slip. The cash, along with the deposit slip, is delivered by the store manager to the bank, and a duplicate copy of the deposit slip is sent to the company's accounting department. The accounting department matches the total cash amount shown on the register tape report with the cash total on the deposit slip and records a debit journal entry in the business's cash account.

Q: Which of our previously listed fraud prevention measures are best exemplified in the preceding example?

» **Segregation of Duties** – The shift manager/supervisor, though he has access to the register tape report, does not have access to the physical cash in the drawer. The cash is delivered directly from the sales clerk to the store manager.

» **Timely Forwarding of Source Documents to Accounting Department** – The accounting department receives both the deposit slip prepared by the store manager and the register tape report prepared by the shift manager/supervisor. Assuming these source documents reconcile with one another, the accounting department will make a prompt and accurate journal entry.

» **Use of Locks and Passwords on Sensitive Documents** – Limited access to the register tape report deters sales clerks from tampering with the cash count.

Were we to add a few hiring controls (background checks, bonding) to our process controls, then we would further diminish the risk of fraud.

NOTE

Another best practice for cash-based businesses is to ensure that the register displays a customer-facing sales total. When the sale is rung up at the register, the customer should see the total in the display. This simple measure prevents employees from overcharging customers for their purchases and pocketing the difference.

In most any cash business involving frequent transactions on a regular basis, there will still be cash discrepancies from time to time, even when meticulous controls are in place. Accountants use "cash over" (revenue) and "cash short" (expense) to account for cash discrepancies.

Assume the register tape from our previous example shows a collection of $2,430 in cash revenues for a given day. The deposit slip, however, shows only $2,425. The register was $5 under. The accounting department would debit the cash account by the amount on the deposit slip ($2,425), but would still record $2,430 sales revenue in the revenue account.

fig. 85

ACCOUNT	DEBIT	CREDIT
Cash	2,425	
Cash Short (expense)	5	
Sales Revenue		2,430

To account for the $5 discrepancy, a $5 expense account entry is debited. Now debits are equal to credits and all is well, so long as these types of shortages or overages do not occur too regularly or in significant sums.

Reconciling Bank Statements

In addition to the handling of incoming cash payments, businesses rely on a multitude of other measures to ensure the integrity of their transactions. Many businesses have a policy that demands a corroborating invoice be created for every check the company issues. Businesses often insist that all checks be filled out by computer using indelible (non-erasable) ink. Employees responsible for making day-to-day purchases are often required to use the company credit card, thereby creating a corroborating record of all transactions. Some businesses have petty cash funds for small items such as taxi fares, business lunches, and other expenses too "petty" to warrant a formal invoice or a check written in indelible ink.

While all of these ideas have the potential to reduce fraud, make the business run smoother, or both, none of them are quite as essential as the periodic reconciliation of a business's books with the records maintained by its bank. A policy of routine **bank reconciliation** gives businesses a chance not to only detect and rectify any bank errors, but also to sniff out any fraud that may be transpiring. The bank statement is where you will find checks that were issued by the business without attached invoices or any record in accounting journals (many times such a finding ends up being attributed to a breakdown in protocol rather than fraud, but if nothing else it provides a space to reemphasize company policy). Sometimes bank reconciliations may reveal that unauthorized withdrawals have been made from company accounts or that checks have been improperly duplicated or altered.

The process of regular bank reconciliation also gives businesses a chance to examine their cash flow through their bank account(s) and to prevent any unwanted overdraft or bounced check fees. And then, of course, there is always the chance of discovering a bank error.

The process of reconciling your accounts is fairly simple, though there are a few minor complexities to be aware of. The appropriate time interval between reconciliations varies from business to business, but generally, once a month, every 30 days or so, makes for a good interval. It may be easiest to reconcile each bank statement in full shortly after it is published online or mailed to you. Go through each transaction on the bank statement and match it up with a corresponding journal entry. Keep in mind that some checks the business has already issued may not have been cashed by the payee, and some checks deposited by the business may not show up on the current bank statement, especially if they were deposited toward the end of the statement period. Nevertheless, these discrepancies should be easy to account for and should not raise any red flags. In fact, the formal procedure for reconciling a bank statement is to account for both deposits in transit and outstanding checks (on the bank statement side). Similarly, on the company bookkeeping side, adjustments should be made to account for any unrecorded items that are already visible on the bank statement. For instance, if a vendor charged a service fee that never made it into the business's books but shows up on the bank statement, then the books should be updated to reflect the expense of the service fee.

By making the necessary adjustments on both sides of the reconciliation, you should come up with the *true* cash balance. The true cash balance reflected in the company's books should be equal to the true cash balance of the bank account. This is a concept that may sound a bit confusing, but is not actually too difficult to understand.

Let's revisit our favorite small business owner, Kathi, owner of Kathi's Jewelry Design. Rather than farm the work out to her accountant, Kathi enjoys reconciling her own bank statement every month after it is issued on the fifteenth. On November 15, Kathi's bank statement balance is $11,910, but the cash balance shown on her cash (asset account) is $11,150. Why the discrepancy?

Bank Statement Balance	$	11,910	Cash (asset account) balance	$	11,150
Deposits in Transit	$	100	Deposits Not Recorded on Books	$	360
Outstanding Checks	$	(715)	Payments Not Recorded on Books	$	(215)
Bank Errors	$	-	Book Errors	$	-
True Bank Balance	$	11,295	**True Book Balance**	$	11,295

In reality, the bank account statement balance and the balance of the cash account on the books will hardly ever be equal right out of the gate, especially not if the business has a regular inflow and outflow of cash. In Kathi's case, though her bank statement balance was $11,910, she had deposited a $100 check the previous evening (the fourteenth) at her bank's night drop deposit station. It will take at least one full day for the deposit to show up. This is known as a "deposit in transit." Deposits in transit must be added to the bank statement balance in order to arrive at the true bank balance. Kathi also has two checks outstanding, one to a utility company and the other to one of her vendors. The total value of the two checks is $715 and is already recorded in the business's books. Therefore, Kathi has $715 in outstanding checks. She must subtract this amount from the bank statement balance in order to arrive at the true bank balance. Kathi is not aware of any bank errors, but if she were, those too would be incorporated into the true bank balance. In order to arrive at the true bank balance, a bank error in Kathi's favor would be subtracted from the bank statement balance, and a bank error in the bank's favor would be added to the statement balance. Kathi calculates her true bank balance at $11,295.

Now let's look at Kathi's books. She has a cash balance of $11,150, but after looking over her bank statement she notices that there is $360 in online sales from last week that have yet to be added to her books. She also notices that there is one payment shown on the bank statement that never made it to the books, a $215 bill paid by Kathi via debit card to a plumbing service that did some work in her store. That expense will ultimately be paid by the landlord, but it is still a technical oversight on Kathi's part; since it was paid using the company checking account, the transaction should have been recorded in the books.

Other than the unrecorded payment, there are no bookkeeping errors that Kathi is made aware of during her reconciliation work. If there were, then she would have to account for them in order to arrive at her true book balance. After adding unrecorded deposits and subtracting unrecorded payments, Kathi calculates her true book balance at $11,295, thereby reconciling her accounting records with her bank statement for the current period.

NOTE

It is preferable that employees who do not handle cash be in charge of reconciling bank accounts. When the same party or parties who handle cash are also responsible for reconciling bank accounts, it creates an opportunity for fraud.

Chapter Recap

» Businesses, especially smaller businesses, victimized by employee fraud can suffer substantial, even devastating, financial losses.

» For an employee to commit fraud, some degree of the following three factors must be present: opportunity, rationalization, and financial pressure.

» The risk of fraud can be reduced through the institution of controls, such as the segregation and rotation of employee duties and the pre-numbering of checks and invoices.

» Strict controls on cash-handling within a business can significantly reduce fraud opportunity.

» Bank reconciliation provides an opportunity to check and perfect records, all while rooting out fraudulent activity.

| 10 |

Sizing Up the Software

Chapter Overview
» Why Software Selection Matters
» Optimal Implementation Times
» Key Considerations

For students of accounting pursuing coursework or a degree of some kind, understanding the underlying mechanics and theories of accounting is unavoidable. You must know how to use debits and credits, ledgers, and the fundamental accounting equation (assets = liabilities + equity). Hopefully, this book has provided you with a strong foundation for your academic pursuits. Other readers, however, may not have any intention of pursuing a degree in accounting or any degree at all. They may be reading this book simply for the purpose of gaining a better grasp of their business's finances. If this is you, then there is a good chance that at some point while reading this book, you thought, *Sheesh, I wonder if it's worth my time to learn all this. Can't QuickBooks do all this stuff for me?*

The truth is that QuickBooks and other accounting software products do a great job taking care of a lot of the internal accounting mechanics. They make it easier to set up, organize, and visualize your accounts, and they will relieve you of much of the tedious calculation. Nevertheless, if you are looking to make a CFO-caliber impact on your business, a knowledge of basic accounting principles in addition to good software is the perfect mix. Then again, you can still find those small business owners out there who, possessing a good fundamental knowledge of accounting, find it simpler to eschew any software and instead rely on the four-filing-cabinet system that we briefly described in chapter 5—one cabinet for assets, one for liabilities, one for revenue/expense, and one for owner capital/withdrawals. After all, software or no software, businesses need to keep some physical documents in order to maintain proper tax compliance and minimize fraud risk. In a good digital/hardcopy hybrid set-up, the software is used to expedite journal entries and the formation of reports, but many tangible hard copy records, such as receipts, purchase orders, and invoices, are kept in the filing system.

According to Linda Pinson, author of *Keeping the Books: Basic Recordkeeping and Accounting for the Successful Small Business*,[15] "One of the mistakes businesses make when they buy accounting software is in believing that they don't need to know anything at all about financial accounting because the software will just take care of it for you." A lot of the fundamental principles in this book, including charts of accounts, debits and credits, and others, are referenced in accounting software, and while you can still use the software to some extent without knowing these concepts, you will get more mileage out of your software if you possess a solid understanding of certain fundamental accounting principles.

When it is time to choose the best software for your business, recognize that there are many options. Mike Budiac runs a website called FindAccountingSoftware.com[16] that helps businesses locate accounting software that best fits their needs. According to Mr. Budiac, "It's real important to get this right. In a lot of cases, it can make the difference between businesses that are profitable versus not profitable."[17]

An Indispensable Resource

The time-saving advantages of accounting software make it an indispensable tool for most modern businesses. In my experience, most small business owners are quite narrowly focused on their tax liability, and they view tax preparation and tax accuracy (deduction tracking and so forth) as the principal utility of their accounting software. Businesses with employees are heavily dependent on their accounting software for payroll processing. Business owners who are also readers of this book are in a privileged position. As mentioned, you can squeeze a lot of extra value out your software when you understand accounting fundamentals. Most accounting software relies on traditional double-entry accounting systems. When journal entries are made in the software—either automatically or manually—at least one account is always debited, and at least one account is equally credited. Income statements, balance sheets, statements of cash flow, and others can all be generated at the touch of a button. Sales reports, cost analyses, and many other highly customized managerial accounting reports can be generated instantly as well. Those who understand accounting fundamentals, whether they are owners, co-owners, or everyday employees, will quickly recognize many of the reporting formats available and be able to make optimal use of them.

An example of the convenience that can be gained from good accounting software is shown in the handling of interest payable expenses generated by business loans. If you recall from chapter 4, interest payable is a liability that accumulates regularly during the life of a loan. Since most loans levy interest charges on a month-by-month basis, usually in accordance with some kind of complex amortization schedule, proper accounting requires a debit to the expense account and a credit to the interest payable account every time interest is assessed. Similarly, when payments are made on the loan, the cash account is credited and both the notes payable and interest payable accounts are debited. Accounting software allows businesses to automate these journal entries, ensuring that interest payable expenses are reflected on financial statements and deducted out of net profit (so as to reduce tax liability)—and it's all done without the tedium of manual entry.

Most accounting software programs are capable of communicating with your bank and credit cards online and importing data and transaction records from these accounts, which you or your accountant will later categorize. Some programs allow you to establish rules for specific transactions. For example, if Becky our donut shop owner was using accounting software, she would want to create a rule dictating that all payments going to Maverick's (the supply company) are automatically debited into supplies (asset) and credited into accounts receivable (liability). In any given month there will be some transactions requiring personal review, but many can be automated.

The Solution Selection Process

In my experience as a CPA I have come to believe that, due in large part to critical tax responsibilities, businesses must choose one or more of three options when handling their accounting.

» **OPTION 1:** Use basic spreadsheet software like Microsoft Excel or Google Sheets. Spreadsheets can quickly perform the arithmetical functions required for basic accounting, but they must be designed, formatted, and maintained.

Using spreadsheets for your accounting needs may be slightly less expensive than using accounting software. But keep in mind that spreadsheets must be programmed and formatted, which requires a significant degree of skill. If you rely on an employee who possesses only mediocre spreadsheet skills, things can get very disorganized very quickly. Worse still, you may end up producing inaccurate records that can distort your business decision-making and get you into tax trouble.

» **OPTION 2:** Choose software appropriate for the needs of the business. When I recommend software to my clients, I usually send them straight to the cloud—I recommend cloud-based software options. From what I have observed, more and more resources are going toward perfecting cloud-based accounting software, whereas desktop software is languishing.

» **OPTION 3:** Outsource all accounting and bookkeeping needs to a third party. Professional accountants and firms can pretty much manage the entirety of your business's accounting and tax needs, end to end. Online bookkeeping firms, such as Bench (bench.co) and my own practice, CPAonFire.com, offer affordable remote accounting services.

I have excluded the use of handwritten ledgers from this list, but there are in fact still some small business owners who get by just fine managing their accounting via pencil, paper, and calculator.

Since this chapter is devoted to businesses choosing the second option, let's take a look at some of the scenarios that induce a business decision-maker to invest in accounting software.

1. **The business is just beginning.** If you are just beginning to cut your teeth as an entrepreneur, then it is best to get your accounting software set up sooner rather than later. Businesses that opt to establish their accounting in spreadsheets or on handwritten ledgers at the beginning will find it more difficult and time-consuming to relay data into a software program at a later date. You are better off just using the software from the beginning. Even if you decide to switch to a different program down the line, you will find that your data is much more portable than it would have been had you opted to use spreadsheets or handwritten ledgers.

2. **The business is beginning to grow.** Though it is possible for a very small business to get by without using accounting software at all, if your business begins to grow at a rapid pace you will probably want to consider enlisting software to aid in the scaling process. It is much easier to scale up with software than to scale up with spreadsheets or handwritten ledgers.

3. **The business needs to streamline functions.** If a lot of time is being wasted performing tasks that can and should be streamlined, then accounting software may be just what the doctor (or the accountant)

ordered. The implementation of accounting software provides an opportunity to hybridize various critical business functions, such as payroll, taxes, and financial reporting. Use your software judiciously and it can add miles to your productivity.

4. **The business is facing an audit or other legal concerns.** A lot of small business owners turn to accounting software when looking to respond to a potential audit or legal concern.

Although good accounting software can help organize and clarify your records, if you are facing an audit, are worried that you might be breaking the law, or are unsure of whether or not you owe a tax penalty, then you are better off consulting with a real licensed accountant.

5. **Business employees need mobile access to accounting records.**
6. Unfortunately, you cannot carry around physical filing cabinets in your pockets. And emailing spreadsheets that are frequently updated is never a good idea. Most accounting software gives users the option of accessing company data and generating up-to-date reports from their mobile phones. If mobility of accounting data is important to your business, then be sure to try out your software's mobile capabilities during that all-important trial period.

If you do decide to use spreadsheets rather than software, consider using a file hosting service such as Google Drive that will allow updates to be made by multiple parties in real time while ensuring that the most recent records are always accessible.

Now that you are aware of some of the business conditions that may trigger the adoption of accounting software, it is important to take note of the factors involved in selecting the optimal software for your business. Here are some of the main factors to consider:

» How computer-literate is the business owner or the employee who will be using the software? Can he handle some complexity, or is it best to give preference to simplicity even if it means sacrificing some functionality?

» Are you comfortable running your accounting software and storing your records in a cloud-based (remote) site? As I mentioned, this is the direction I foresee for the accounting software industry. Many noteworthy names in accounting software, such as QuickBooks, NetBooks, NetSuite, and Clarity Accounting, have launched online-only versions of their products. These services often charge very affordable monthly subscription fees. Though cloud servers are sure to be nominally as secure as your local office network, or more so, you are nonetheless entrusting your data to an entity beyond your own direct control. Are you ready to step into the future?

» How much can your business afford to spend? Many of the basic-package accounting software options have a reasonable entry-level price point, but once you start getting into industry-specific, specialized programs, the price can spike dramatically. As a best practice, inspect and consider the various service-level tiers offered by each software program.

» What type of business do you operate? A lot of different accounting programs have specific versions or add-on modules that accommodate certain business types. Remember, if your business manufactures children's toys, its accounting needs will vary from those of a physician's conglomerate.

» What are the limits of your business's hardware capacity? Some of these accounting programs are real bruisers when it comes to sucking up computing resources. Check with your IT department to get an idea of what is possible with your current configurations.

» What additional non-accounting functionality does the business want included with its accounting software? Would it benefit from an add-on point-of-sale program or a customer relationship management add-on? Many accounting software publishers, such as QuickBooks, offer deluxe products that bundle in several business software services, beyond just accounting.

Another option when selecting software is to temporarily hire an accountant or accounting firm. If you have a broader need for financial stabilization at your company, then software advice may prove to be one of many benefits you gain from professional support.

It might also be fruitful to ask around, either in person or in online forums, to find out what other businesses—that have financial realities similar to yours—are using for accounting software. Read reviews in magazines and online.

A final word of common-sense advice: make the most of your risk-free trial period. Any competitor in the accounting software space who wants to be taken seriously will give you the chance to try the product risk-free. Part of the calculation, of course, is that once your financial records are well-entwined with the software—once you have linked all of your bank accounts, credit cards, etc.—then the last thing you will want to do is to go back through the entire set-up process with another program. Nonetheless, if your needs are not met by the first software you try out, and you believe you will fare better with a different product, do not hesitate to exercise your rights under the trial period.

Choosing the right (or any) software solution requires research and will be guided by the unique characteristics of your business: the industry, the size, and the amount you want to spend on software. The ideas and speculation points in this chapter are intended to prime your decision-making process with good food for thought. At some point, though, you must turn to the market at large and do your best to make the optimal decision for your business. Good luck!

Chapter Recap

» Most modern businesses—small, medium, and large—depend on accounting software.

» Accounting software does not neutralize the value of a strong knowledge of accounting principles.

» Basic tax requirements necessitate the implementation of some form of financial accounting; businesses tend to rely on either spreadsheets, accounting software, or outsourcing to professionals.

» When using professional accounting services on a temporary basis (i.e., for tax season), ask someone to recommend a software program appropriate for your business.

Conclusion

Congratulations! If you have made it all the way through this book, then you are several steps ahead of fellow students, other business owners, and other bookkeepers and managers. Many of the concepts that we have introduced will undoubtedly require practice. Like any other language, the language of business, aka accounting, is best learned through total immersion. Whether you are in an office or classroom environment, *practice makes perfect* is the law of the land. You students will have a bit of an advantage here, in that you will be sufficiently motivated by your instructors to complete your homework assignments on time and to study for your exams. Business owners, bookkeepers, and finance managers may need to exert a greater degree of self-discipline in order to internalize these fundamental accounting concepts so that they become second nature. To help you on your way to mastery, we have included a twelve-question Bonus Quiz that can be found on page 173 I would also recommend the following tips for you business owners and managers who are serious about applying the power of accounting principles to your business.

> » **Define your financial statement periods**. Decide whether you want to generate your financial statements once a quarter, once a month, once a week, etc. If you are working with software, then it should be quite easy to print your statements on demand. The tricky part is ensuring that all relevant receipts, bank records, and other source documents have been accurately entered into the system.

> » **Spend some time thinking about and setting up your financial filing system**. Recall from chapter 5 that a basic accounting filing system requires only four filing cabinets, one for assets, one for liabilities, one for equity accounts (revenues and expenses), and the last for the owner's capital accounts. You can use these cabinets to store receipts, loan records, invoices, and other source documents, while also storing copies of your periodic financial statements.

» **Consider hiring temporary financial management support.** Many businesses reach a predicament, often when tax season approaches, where they realize they are in need of some specialized financial support but are not quite comfortable with hiring on a full-time bookkeeper or CFO. Many part-time CFO and bookkeeping services are available to service this common need. Business owners and managers like you, who are endeavoring to learn accounting fundamentals, will likely gain lasting benefits from even just a few weeks of professional support. Once your temporary financial consultant gets the ball rolling, you will be in a good position to carry it forward.

» **Use cash basis accounting if it is a better fit for your business.** Though this book focuses more on the formal accrual-basis approach to accounting, many smaller businesses will find that cash basis accounting is simply easier to manage. Revenues are recorded only when the business receives cash payments, and expenses are recorded only when cash departs the business. Almost all the other accounting principles from this book can still be easily applied. Keep in mind that the IRS will only permit businesses to use cash accounting if their annual revenues are less than $10 million *and* even if the revenue threshold is met, businesses that keep inventories are still usually required to use an accrual basis to account for their inventory expense.

» **Make sure you understand the totality of your tax obligations.** Though our tax chapter (chapter 8) in this book focuses primarily on business income tax, taxes come in many forms and are assessed by many different government entities. Retailers must be sure to collect and pay sales tax. Importers are often required to pay "use" tax. Counties collect property taxes. States collect state income taxes. Understanding and planning for the totality of the tax burden is essential for a financially conscious business owner.

Thanks for reading, and best of luck to you!

REMEMBER TO DOWNLOAD
YOUR FREE DIGITAL ASSETS!

 Sample Financial Statement Templates

 Helpful Accounting Ratio Cheat Sheet

 Business Plan Creation Tools for Entrepreneurs

 Easy Tax Treatment Cheat Sheet

TWO WAYS TO ACCESS YOUR FREE DIGITAL ASSETS

Use the camera app on your mobile phone to scan the QR code
or visit the link below and instantly access your digital assets.

 SCAN ME or www.clydebankmedia.com/accounting-assets 🖥 **VISIT URL**

Bonus Quiz

Match the account described to the account type (Questions 1–8).

Case 1: A Real Estate Conglomerate

Questions 1 through 4 pertain to the accounting used at a real estate conglomerate, the Sampson Group, which hires the Coast Property Management Company to oversee its many rental properties.

1. What type of account does the Sampson Group use to report rental payments from tenants?

   a) Asset   b) Liability   c) Expense   d) Revenue   e) Equity

2. When the Sampson Group first formed, they raised capital by issuing 5-year and 10-year bonds. Interest paid on the bonds is considered an expense. What type of account is used to track the remaining principal payments due to service the bond?

   a) Asset   b) Liability   c) Expense   d) Revenue   e) Equity

3. The Sampson Group purchased a vehicle in the company's name so the owners could write off gas mileage for business trips. The company purchases an auto insurance policy to cover the vehicle. What type of account is used to keep track of vehicle insurance premiums paid?

   a) Asset   b) Liability   c) Expense   d) Revenue   e) Equity

4. The apartments in one of the Sampson Group's properties experienced a wave of vandalism. In response, the Gold Coast Property Management Company quickly purchased and set up a new security system with additional lighting and security cameras. Gold Coast sent the bill for the new security system to the Sampson Group but it is not due until the following month. Using accrual-based accounting, what type of account is immediately debited when recording the price of the new security system? What type of account is credited?

a) Cash (asset account) is debited; Security (asset account) is credited

b) Expense is debited; Accounts payable (liability account) is credited

c) Expense is credited; Security (asset account) is debited

d) Accounts receivable (asset account) is debited; Revenue is credited

e) Accounts payable (liability account) is debited; Revenue is credited

Case 2: Sail Away Boat Tours

Questions 5 through 8 pertain to the accounts of a private touring company that operates in the Florida Keys.

5. Sail Away Boat Tours has a fleet of twelve boats that cost, on average, $35,000 each. Over the course of five years the value of these boats depreciates. To account for the depreciation, the company's assets are credited. Which account type is debited?

a) Asset   b) Liability   c) Expense   d) Revenue   e) Equity

6. After being in operation for 20 years, the original owners of Sail Away Boat Tours sell the entire company to a mysterious multimillionaire who has plans for rapidly expanding the business. Using his own money, the new owner immediately adds one million dollars to the company's cash coffers. Which account type is credited when this influx of capital is recorded?

a) Asset   b) Liability   c) Expense   d) Revenue   e) Equity

7. The necessary licensure is obtained and Sail Away Boat Tours is now authorized to sell beer and liquor on the boat during tours. The company managers order $5,000 worth of alcohol and keep it in storage. What type of account would be used to track the value of the alcohol on hand?

a) Asset (inventory)   d) Revenue (sales)

b) Liability (accounts payable)   e) Equity (owner's capital)

c) Expense (supplies)

8. Following the mysterious multimillionaire's expansion of the company, he now plans to operate a fleet of 60 boats throughout the Florida Keys and all of south Florida. Two of the new boats, each purchased for $35,000, were lightly damaged in transit. Rather than return the boats, the management at Sail Away Boat Tours asks for

a 10 percent discount ($3,500) on each boat. The boat vendor agrees. Upon receipt of the partial refund, the accountant at Sail Away Boat Tours makes a $7,000 cash debit. Which account type is credited?

a) Asset (inventory)

b) Liability (accounts payable)

c) Expense (supplies)

d) Revenue (sales)

e) Equity (owner's capital)

Case 3: Gunther's Gear Shop

Questions 9 through 12 pertain to the accounts of a camera and studio equipment online retailer.

Former Los Angeles-based set technician, Greg Gunther, decides to go into business for himself. He incorporates (as an S corporation) Gunther's Gear Shop, dedicated to providing affordable supplies to studios big and small.

In order to finance his endeavor, Gunther successfully raises $50,000 through the selling of stock shares to himself and to private investors. He also takes out a bank loan worth $25,000.

His first year in business is 2019. During the course of the year, Gunther's Gear Shop uses cash to purchase $115,000 worth of inventory, and the business makes $185,000 in sales. His total cost of goods sold is $63,000. Some of Gunther's customers are individuals, but many are commercial studios. Of the $185,000 in sales, Gunther receives $155,000 in cash, and the remaining $30,000 is still owed by various customers.

To keep his website up and active during the course of the year, Gunther pays $5,000 (selling expense), with an additional $3,000 spent on advertising and search engine optimization. Gunther has hired two part-time employees and gives himself a small salary. He spends a total of $50,000 on all salaries, including his own. Gunther spends an extra $12,000 on supplies. All of these expenses are paid in cash.

In the middle of the year, Gunther decides to invest $5,000 in a locally hosted server system that will allow him to host all of his ecommerce locally, without having to pay commissions to third parties.

Over the course of the year, Gunther's bank loan incurs $2,000 in interest expense and he pays off $1,000 of the principal. He also pays out $7,500 in dividends to himself and other stockholders during the course of the year.

Gunther's business ends the year with $29,500 cash in the company bank account.

9. Prepare a 2019 income statement for Gunther's Gear Shop.

10. Prepare a 2019 retained earnings statement for Gunther's Gear Shop.

11. Prepare a 2019 balance sheet for Gunther's Gear Shop.

12. Prepare a 2019 statement of cash flows for Gunther's Gear Shop.

ANSWERS ON PAGE 181

About the Author

JOSH BAUERLE, CPA

Josh Bauerle is a CPA and the founder of CPA On Fire, a tax and accounting practice specializing in working with online business owners.

Over the course of his ten-plus years in the industry, Josh has experienced a wide range of roles in the accounting world: cost accountant at a Fortune 500 company, auditor and tax preparer at a public accounting firm, financial advisor and, finally, owner of his own firm. This experience has allowed him to see firsthand the importance of proper accounting at all levels of business, from the billion-dollar companies to the guy starting an Amazon store from his basement.

Since founding CPA On Fire in 2012, Josh has become a sought-after expert in the accounting and tax industry, appearing on some of the largest business podcasts in the country and on national TV shows.

Josh lives in Willard, Ohio, with his wife Courtney, twin boys Jacob and Eli, and daughter Mollie. When he's not helping business owners with accounting, he is coaching the Willard Lady Flashes tennis team, which just completed the school's first-ever undefeated regular season and SBC Championship. mers for a small business, no matter what industry they're in.

About ClydeBank Media

We create simplified educational tools that allow our customers to successfully learn new skills in order to navigate this constantly changing world.

The success of ClydeBank Media's value-driven approach starts with beginner-friendly high-quality information. We work with subject matter experts who are leaders in their fields. These experts are supported by our team of professional researchers, writers, and educators.

Our team at ClydeBank Media works with these industry leaders to break down their wealth of knowledge, their wisdom, and their years of experience into small and concise building blocks. We piece together these building blocks to create a clearly defined learning path that a beginner can follow for successful mastery.

At ClydeBank Media, we see a new world of possibility. Simplified learning doesn't have to be bound by four walls; instead, it's driven by you.

Answers

1) d   2) b   3) c   4) b   5) c   6) e   7) a   8) a

9)

Gunther's Gear Shop
Income Statement
For the Year Ending on 12/31/19

Revenues		
Sales revenue	$ 185,000	
TOTAL REVENUES		$ 185,000
Expenses		
Cost of goods sold expense	$ 63,000	
Salary and wages expense	$ 50,000	
Supplies expense	$ 12,000	
Selling expense	$ 5,000	
Website expense	$ 5,000	
Advertising expense	$ 3,000	
Interest expense	$ 2,000	
TOTAL EXPENSES		$ 140,000
Net income		$ 45,000

10)

Gunther's Gear Shop
Retained Earnings Statement
For the Year Ending on 12/31/19

Retained Earnings as of January 1	$	-
Plus: Net income	$	45,000
	$	45,000
Less: Dividends issued	$	7,500
Retained Earnings as of December 31	$	37,500

11)

Gunther's Gear Shop
Balance Sheet
12/31/19

Assets

Cash	$	29,500
Accounts receivable	$	30,000
Inventory	$	52,000
TOTAL ASSETS	$	111,500

Liabilities and Stockholder Equity

Liabilities

Notes payable	$	24,000	
TOTAL LIABILITIES		$	24,000

Stockholders' Equity

Common stock	$	50,000	
Retained Earnings	$	37,500	
TOTAL EQUITY		$	87,500
TOTAL LIABILITIES PLUS STOCKHOLDERS' EQUITY		$	111,500

12)

Gunther's Gear Shop
Statement of Cash Flows
For the Year Ending on 12/31/19

Cash Flows from Operating Activities		
Cash flows from sales	$ 155,000	
Outgoing cash from operating activities	$ (72,000)	
Inventory purchase (sold)	$ (63,000)	
Inventory purchase (unsold)	$ (52,000)	
NET CASH FLOW FROM OPERATIONS		$ (32,000)
Cash Flows from Investing Activities		
Equipment investment	$ (5,000)	
NET CASH FLOW FROM INVESTING		$ (5,000)
Cash Flows from Financing Activities		
Issuance of common stock	$ 50,000	
Issuance of notes payable	$ 25,000	
Principal payments on notes payable	$ (1,000)	
Dividends paid	$ (7,500)	
NET CASH FLOW FROM FINANCING		$ 66,500
Net Cash Flow		$ 29,500
Cash position at the beginning of the period		$ -
Current cash position		$ 29,500

Glossary

Account
A record that displays the culmination of certain transactions. Every account is classified as an asset, liability, equity value, revenue, or expense.

Accountant
A skilled professional trained to optimally maintain and analyze data, particularly financial data and that relevant to the management of a business or organization.

Accrual basis accounting
An accounting method in which businesses record transactions when services are performed or goods are delivered, regardless of payment timelines.

Adjusting entries
Entries made at the end of an accounting period to ensure that recorded transactions are adequately reflected within all time periods in which they are relevant.

Annual report
A report issued by a company on a yearly basis that includes financial statements, analysis and commentary by management, and an auditor's review.

Average tax rate
Total tax paid expressed as a percentage of total income.

Asset accounts
Accounts that track and quantify the financial value of a company's assets, such as land, property, equipment, inventory, copyrights, patents, or other assets.

Balance sheet
A financial statement that itemizes the value of a business's assets during a specific moment in time and quantifies the claims being made on those assets by creditors and equity holders.

Bank reconciliation
The periodic comparison of a business's books with its bank statements.

Bookkeeper
A person responsible for updating, centralizing, and maintaining accurate records reflecting a business or organization's financial or other accounting data.

Book value
The recorded value of an asset as recorded in a business's books, which includes adjustments for depreciation.

Cash basis accounting
An accounting method in which businesses record transactions on the basis of when cash changes hands.

Certified public accountant (CPA)
A professional accountant licensed to provide accounting services to the general public.

Chart of accounts
A listing of a company's accounts.

Chief financial officer (CFO)
An executive-level employee responsible for a company's financial strategy and reporting.

Contribution margin
The quantity of revenue left over after all variable costs are accounted for.

Cost-volume-profit (CVP) analysis
The study of the interplay between the costs of goods and services, sales quantities, and profit.

Current assets
Assets owned by a business that are expected to be converted to cash and/or consumed entirely within a year's time or within the current operating cycle.

Current liabilities
Debts expected to be paid within a year's time or within the current operating cycle.

Current ratio
Current assets divided by current liabilities; a measure of a company's ability to pay its short-term debts.

Debt-to-asset ratio
Total liabilities divided by total assets; a solvency ratio that describes the extent to which a company's assets are financed by creditors.

Double-entry accounting
A widely used approach to accounting whereby at least two entries are made when recording any given transaction.

Earnings per share (EPS)
The amount of income generated by a company divided by out-standing shares of common stock.

Equity
The ownership claim on the value of an asset (like a business or a house). Equity is reduced by liabilities (like debt) that also exert claims on the value of the same asset; hence, Assets = Liabilities + Equity (or Equity = Assets – Liabilities).

Equity accounts
Accounts that track and quantify equity.

FIFO (first-in, first-out)
An inventory accounting protocol whereby the assumed cost of goods sold is derived from the cost of the product that has been in inventory the longest.

Financial accounting
A specific branch of accounting that focuses on a business's presentation of financial data to interested parties outside of the business, such as stockholders or potential lenders.

Fiscal year
Any twelve-month period that a business chooses to use for tax or accounting purposes.

Free cash flow
Net cash flow from operating activities after capital expenditures and cash dividends are subtracted.

General ledger
A business's listing of accounts and their values that incorporates all asset, liability, and equity accounts used by the business.

Income statement
A financial statement that lists a business's revenues, expenses, and net income for a given time period.

Intangible assets
Assets such as patents, trademarks, copyrights, and trade names that may possess value but lack any physical substance.

Intercompany comparison
The comparison of two or more companies to one another on the basis of earnings per share (EPS) or other metrics.

Intracompany comparison
Evaluation of the performance of a single company over successive time periods.

Journal entry
A notation showing a debit (on the left side) and a credit (on the right side) of accounts affected by a transaction.

Liability accounts
Accounts that track and quantify financial obligations owed to creditors in the form of debts and other obligations.

LIFO (last-in, first-out)
An inventory accounting protocol whereby the assumed cost of goods sold may be derived from the cost of the product that has been in inventory for the shortest amount of time.

Liquidity ratios
Ratios such as current ratio, quick ratio, and cash ratio; used to evaluate a company's ability to meet its short-term financial obligations.

Long-term assets
Assets owned by a business that are not expected to be converted into cash and/or consumed entirely within a year's time or within the current operating cycle.

Long-term liabilities
Debts that are not expected to be paid off until after at least one year's time.

Managerial accounting
A specific branch of accounting that focuses on a business's discrete, strategic, detailed financial and logistical reporting and analysis of day-by-day business activities.

Marginal tax rate
The amount of tax paid on an additional dollar of income.

Matching principle
An important principle in accounting which says that expenses should be reported in the same accounting period as the revenues they helped to earn.

Net income
Total revenues minus total expenses.

Operating cycle
The average time required to purchase inventory, sell it, and collect cash from customers.

Owner's equity
The owner's claim on the assets of a business.

Patent
An intangible asset that grants companies the exclusive, government-guaranteed right to manufacture and sell an invention.

Period costs
Costs that cannot be attributed to the production or delivery of a specific product or service.

Product costs
The costs expended in the creation of a product or the delivery of a service.

Pro forma income
A secondary (non-GAAP) measurement of income that excludes items that the company deems unusual or nonrecurring.

Retained earnings statement
A financial statement that quantifies the amount of net income remaining after dividends are paid to stockholders.

Residual value
A base value beneath which an asset may not be depreciated any further—also known as "salvage value."

Reversing entry
A type of adjusting entry where an entry is made at the end of an accounting period and immediately reversed at the beginning of the next accounting period.

Solvency ratios
Ratios such as the price-to-earnings ratio, price-to-sales ratio, and debt-to-asset ratio, used to evaluate a company's ability to survive over a long period of time.

Source documents
The primary records used to verify that a change must be made to one or more accounts.

Statement of cash flows
A financial statement that clarifies the inflow and outflow of cash over a given time period.

Statement of owner's equity
A financial statement that details the contributions, withdrawals, and equity values of a business's owner or owners.

Sustainable income

Income that, as judged by a business's investors, is likely to be generated by that business on a perpetual basis.

Target income

The amount of money (profit) a business seeks to make in order to attain its financial objectives.

Tax credit

A reduction in total tax owed.

Tax deduction

A reduction in total taxable earnings.

Trial balance

A list of accounts and their balances at a specific time.

Working capital

A company's current assets minus its current liabilities.

References

Kimmel, Paul D., Jerry J. Weygandt and Donald E. Kieso, *Financial Accounting: Tools for Business Decision Making*. Hoboken, New Jersey: John Wiley & Sons, 2016.

Wild, John J., Ken W. Shaw and Barbara Chiappetta, *Fundamental Accounting Principles*. New York, NY: McGraw-Hill Education, 2013.

INTRODUCTION

1   …which is actually a real course offered at the Fashion Institute of Technology in New York.

2   Association of Certified Fraud Examiners, *2014 Global Fraud Study; Report to the Nations on Occupational Fraud and Abuse*, (Austin, TX, 2014). http://www.acfe.com/rttn/docs/2014-report-to-nations.pdf

3   Pew Research Center, "Three-in-Ten U.S. Jobs Are Held by the Self-Employed and the Workers They Hire." PewSocialTrends.org, October 22, 2015, http://www.pewsocialtrends.org/2015/10/22/three-in-ten-u-s-jobs-are-held-by-the-self-employed-and-the-workers-they-hire/

CHAPTER 1

4   ClydeBank Business, *LLC QuickStart Guide: The Simplified Beginner's Guide to Limited Liability Companies*. Albany, NY: ClydeBank Media, 2015.

5   ClydeBank Business, *Taxes for Small Businesses QuickStart Guide: Understanding Taxes for Your Sole Proprietorship, Startup, & LLC*. Albany, NY: ClydeBank Media, 2015.

CHAPTER 3

6   ClydeBank Business, *Investing QuickStart Guide: The Simplified Beginner's Guide to Successfully Navigating the Stock Market, Growing Your Wealth, & Creating a Secure Financial Future*. Albany, NY: ClydeBank Media, 2015.

CHAPTER 4

7   "Balance Sheet for Nintendo," Morningstar, accessed August 30, 2017, http://financials.morningstar.com/balance-sheet/bs.html?t=NTDOY.

8   "Financial Statements for United Parcel Service, Inc." Google Finance, accessed August 30, 2017, https://www.google.com/finance?q=NYSE%3AUPS&fstype=ii&ei=G7VKWYHoB4H2jAHi8Kb4BA

9   Ibid.

CHAPTER 6

10   All software products listed are currently on the market at the time of this writing, with verified 2017 updates.

CHAPTER 7

11   John J. Wild, Ken W. Shaw and Barbara Chiappetta, *Fundamental Accounting Principles*. (New York, NY: McGraw-Hill, 2013).

12   ClydeBank Business, *Investing QuickStart Guide: The Simplified Beginner's Guide to Successfully Navigating the Stock Market, Growing Your Wealth, & Creating a Secure Financial Future.* Albany, NY: ClydeBank Media, 2015.

CHAPTER 9

13   Kroll, "The Threat Within: Insider Fraud on the Rise," November 23, 2015, https://www.kroll.com/en-us/intelligence-center/press-releases/the-threat-within-insider-fraud-on-the-rise

14   Association of Certified Fraud Examiners, *2016 Global Fraud Study; Report to the Nations on Occupational Fraud and Abuse*, (Austin, TX, 2016). https://www.acfe.com/rttn2016/docs/2016-report-to-the-nations.pdf

CHAPTER 10

15   Pinson, Linda. *Keeping the Books: Basic Recordkeeping and Accounting for the Successful Small Business.* (Chicago: Dearborn Trade Publishing, 2004).

16   This URL now redirects users to https://softwareconnect.com/accounting/ which appears to offer essentially the same service.

17   Elizabeth Wasserman, "How to Choose Business Accounting Software." Inc.com, accessed August 30, 2017, http://www.inc.com/guides/choosing-accounting-software.html

Index

Notes

WHAT DID YOU THINK?

We rely on reviews and reader feedback to help our authors reach more people, improve our books, and grow our business. We would really appreciate it if you took the time to help us out by providing feedback on your recent purchase.

It's really easy, it only takes a second, and it's a tremendous help!

── NOT SURE WHAT TO SHARE? ──
Here are some ideas to get your review started…

- *What did you learn?*
- *Have you been able to put anything you learned into action?*
- *Would you recommend the book to other readers?*
- *Is the author clear and easy to understand?*

TWO WAYS TO LEAVE AN AMAZON REVIEW

Use the camera app on your mobile phone to scan the QR code or visit the link below to record your testimonial and get your free book.

or

www.quickstartguides.review/accounting

📱 SCAN ME   🖥 VISIT URL

GET YOUR NEXT
QuickStart Guide®
FOR FREE

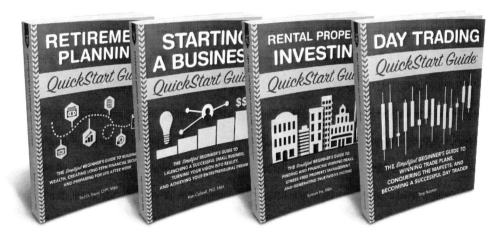

Leave us a quick video testimonial on our website and we will give you a **FREE *QuickStart Guide*** of your choice!

RECORD TESTIMONIAL　　　**SUBMIT TO OUR WEBSITE**　　　**GET A FREE BOOK**

SAVE 10% ON YOUR NEXT

QuickStart Guide®

USE CODE: QSG10

www.quickstartguides.shop/business

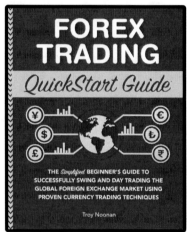

www.quickstartguides.shop/forex

www.quickstartguides.shop/investing

www.quickstartguides.shop/html-css

Use the camera app on your mobile phone to scan the QR code or visit the link below the cover to shop.

Get 10% off your entire order when you use code 'QSG10' at checkout at www.clydebankmedia.com

CLYDEBANK MEDIA

QuickStart Guides®

PROUDLY SUPPORT ONE TREE PLANTED

One Tree Planted is a 501(c)(3) nonprofit organization focused on global reforestation, with millions of trees planted every year. ClydeBank Media is proud to support One Tree Planted as a reforestation partner.

Every dollar donated plants one tree and every tree makes a difference!

Learn more at www.clydebankmedia.com/charitable-giving or make a contribution at onetreeplanted.org

Made in United States
North Haven, CT
24 September 2022

24509276R00117